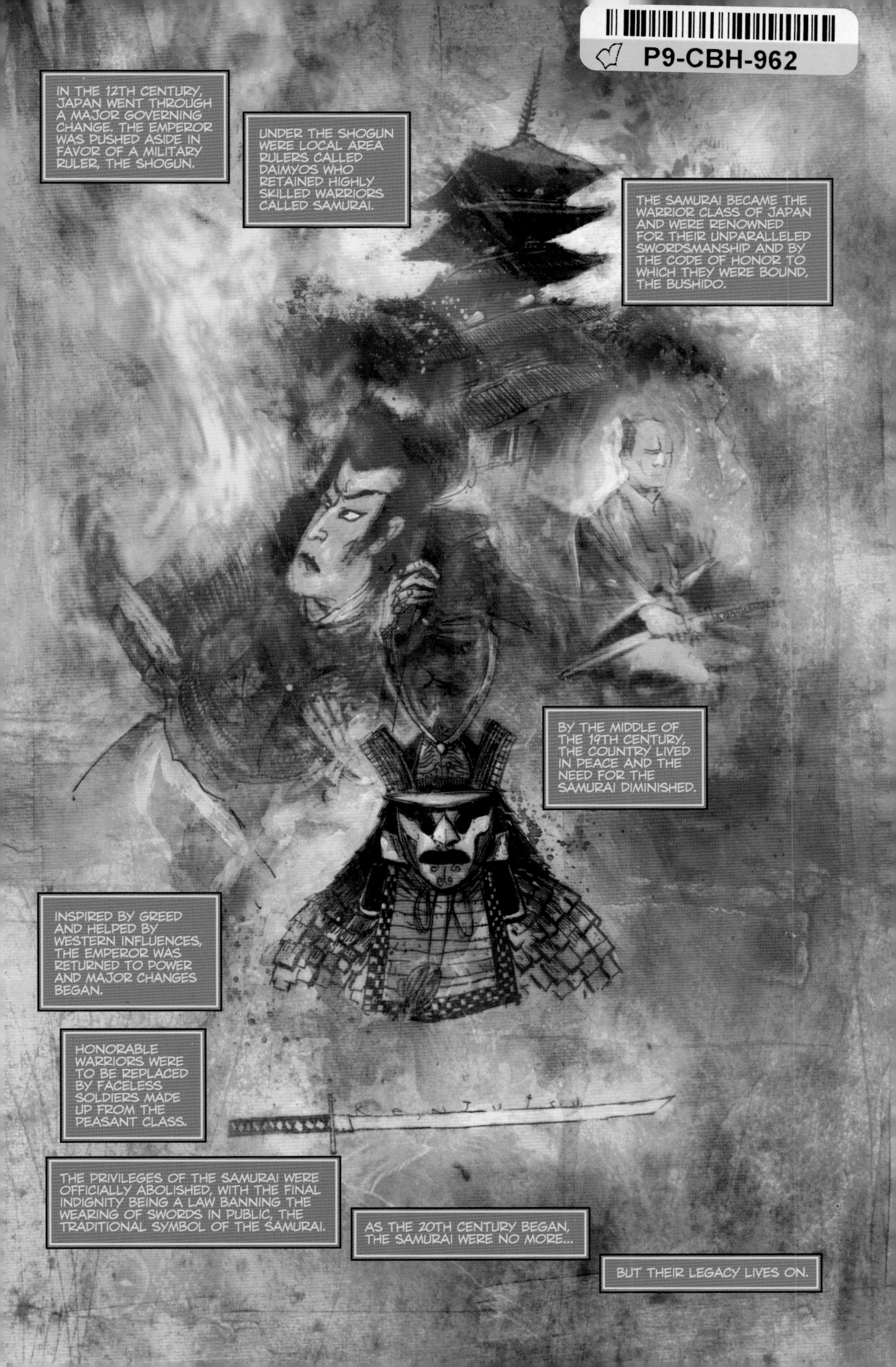
IN THE 12TH CENTURY, JAPAN WENT THROUGH A MAJOR GOVERNING CHANGE. THE EMPEROR WAS PUSHED ASIDE IN FAVOR OF A MILITARY RULER, THE SHOGUN.
UNDER THE SHOGUN WERE LOCAL AREA RULERS CALLED DAIMYOS WHO RETAINED HIGHLY SKILLED WARRIORS CALLED SAMURAI.
THE SAMURAI BECAME THE WARRIOR CLASS OF JAPAN AND WERE RENOWNED FOR THEIR UNPARALLELED SWORDSMANSHIP AND BY THE CODE OF HONOR TO WHICH THEY WERE BOUND, THE BUSHIDO.
BY THE MIDDLE OF THE 19TH CENTURY, THE COUNTRY LIVED IN PEACE AND THE NEED FOR THE SAMURAI DIMINISHED.
INSPIRED BY GREED AND HELPED BY WESTERN INFLUENCES, THE EMPEROR WAS RETURNED TO POWER AND MAJOR CHANGES BEGAN.
HONORABLE WARRIORS WERE TO BE REPLACED BY FACELESS SOLDIERS MADE UP FROM THE PEASANT CLASS.
KENJUTSU
THE PRIVILEGES OF THE SAMURAI WERE OFFICIALLY ABOLISHED, WITH THE FINAL INDIGNITY BEING A LAW BANNING THE WEARING OF SWORDS IN PUBLIC, THE TRADITIONAL SYMBOL OF THE SAMURAI.
AS THE 20TH CENTURY BEGAN, THE SAMURAI WERE NO MORE...
BUT THEIR LEGACY LIVES ON.

A HANDFUL OF PEOPLE STILL BELIEVE IN THE WAYS OF THE SAMURAI. THEY STILL TRAIN THEIR CHILDREN TO FOLLOW THE SEVEN PRINCIPLES OF BUSHIDO.

gi
justice, making the right decision.

yu
courage, bravery tinged with heroism.

jin
benevolence, universal love towards mankind.

rei
respect, courtesy to your elders and superiors.

makoto
honesty, to be truthful at all times.

meiyo
honor, living up to one's moral beliefs.

chugi
loyalty, faithful to one's master or parents.

BUT IN A WORLD WHERE CORPORATIONS HAVE REPLACED CLANS AND GREED HAS CIRCUMVENTED HONOR, THOSE WHO FOLLOW THE WAY OF THE WARRIOR ARE FAR TOO FEW.

KENJI!

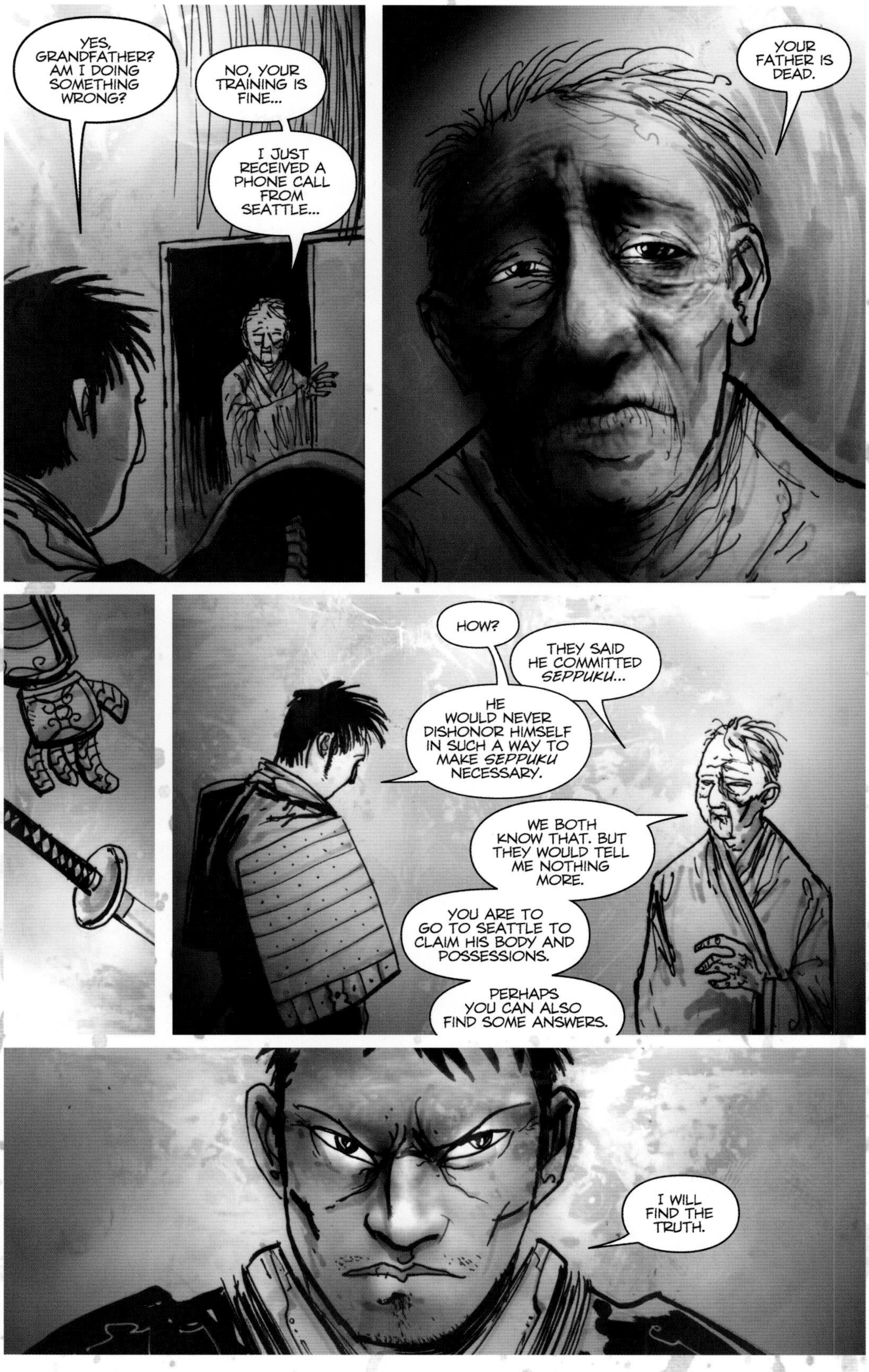
YES, GRANDFATHER? AM I DOING SOMETHING WRONG?
NO, YOUR TRAINING IS FINE...
I JUST RECEIVED A PHONE CALL FROM SEATTLE...
YOUR FATHER IS DEAD.
HOW?
THEY SAID HE COMMITTED *SEPPUKU*...
HE WOULD NEVER DISHONOR HIMSELF IN SUCH A WAY TO MAKE *SEPPUKU* NECESSARY.
WE BOTH KNOW THAT. BUT THEY WOULD TELL ME NOTHING MORE.
YOU ARE TO GO TO SEATTLE TO CLAIM HIS BODY AND POSSESSIONS.
PERHAPS YOU CAN ALSO FIND SOME ANSWERS.
I WILL FIND THE TRUTH.

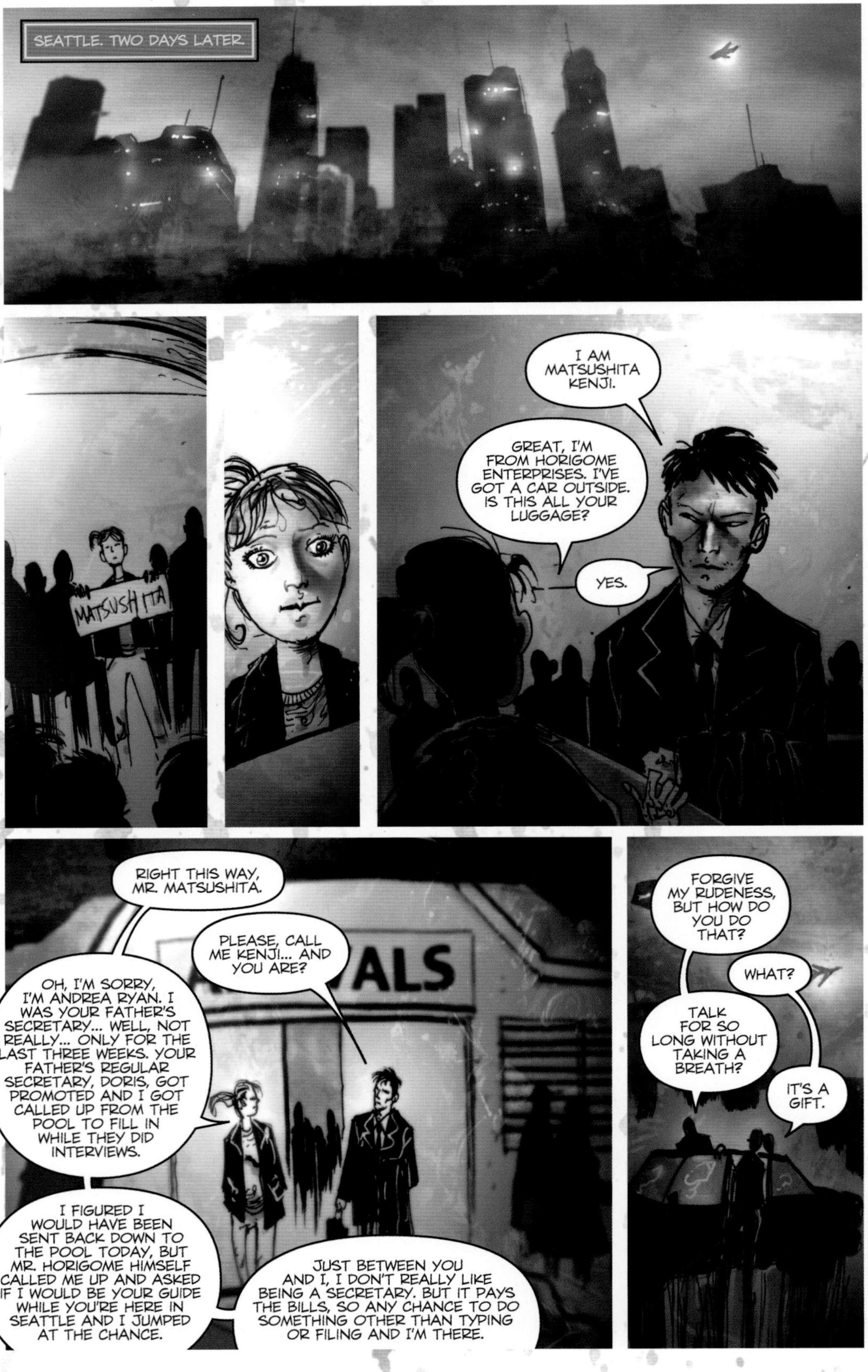
SEATTLE. TWO DAYS LATER.
MATSUSHITA
I AM MATSUSHITA KENJI.
GREAT, I'M FROM HORIGOME ENTERPRISES. I'VE GOT A CAR OUTSIDE. IS THIS ALL YOUR LUGGAGE?
YES.
RIGHT THIS WAY, MR. MATSUSHITA.
PLEASE, CALL ME KENJI... AND YOU ARE?
OH, I'M SORRY, I'M ANDREA RYAN. I WAS YOUR FATHER'S SECRETARY... WELL, NOT REALLY... ONLY FOR THE LAST THREE WEEKS. YOUR FATHER'S REGULAR SECRETARY, DORIS, GOT PROMOTED AND I GOT CALLED UP FROM THE POOL TO FILL IN WHILE THEY DID INTERVIEWS.
I FIGURED I WOULD HAVE BEEN SENT BACK DOWN TO THE POOL TODAY, BUT MR. HORIGOME HIMSELF CALLED ME UP AND ASKED IF I WOULD BE YOUR GUIDE WHILE YOU'RE HERE IN SEATTLE AND I JUMPED AT THE CHANCE.
JUST BETWEEN YOU AND I, I DON'T REALLY LIKE BEING A SECRETARY. BUT IT PAYS THE BILLS, SO ANY CHANCE TO DO SOMETHING OTHER THAN TYPING OR FILING AND I'M THERE.
FORGIVE MY RUDENESS, BUT HOW DO YOU DO THAT?
WHAT?
TALK FOR SO LONG WITHOUT TAKING A BREATH?
IT'S A GIFT.

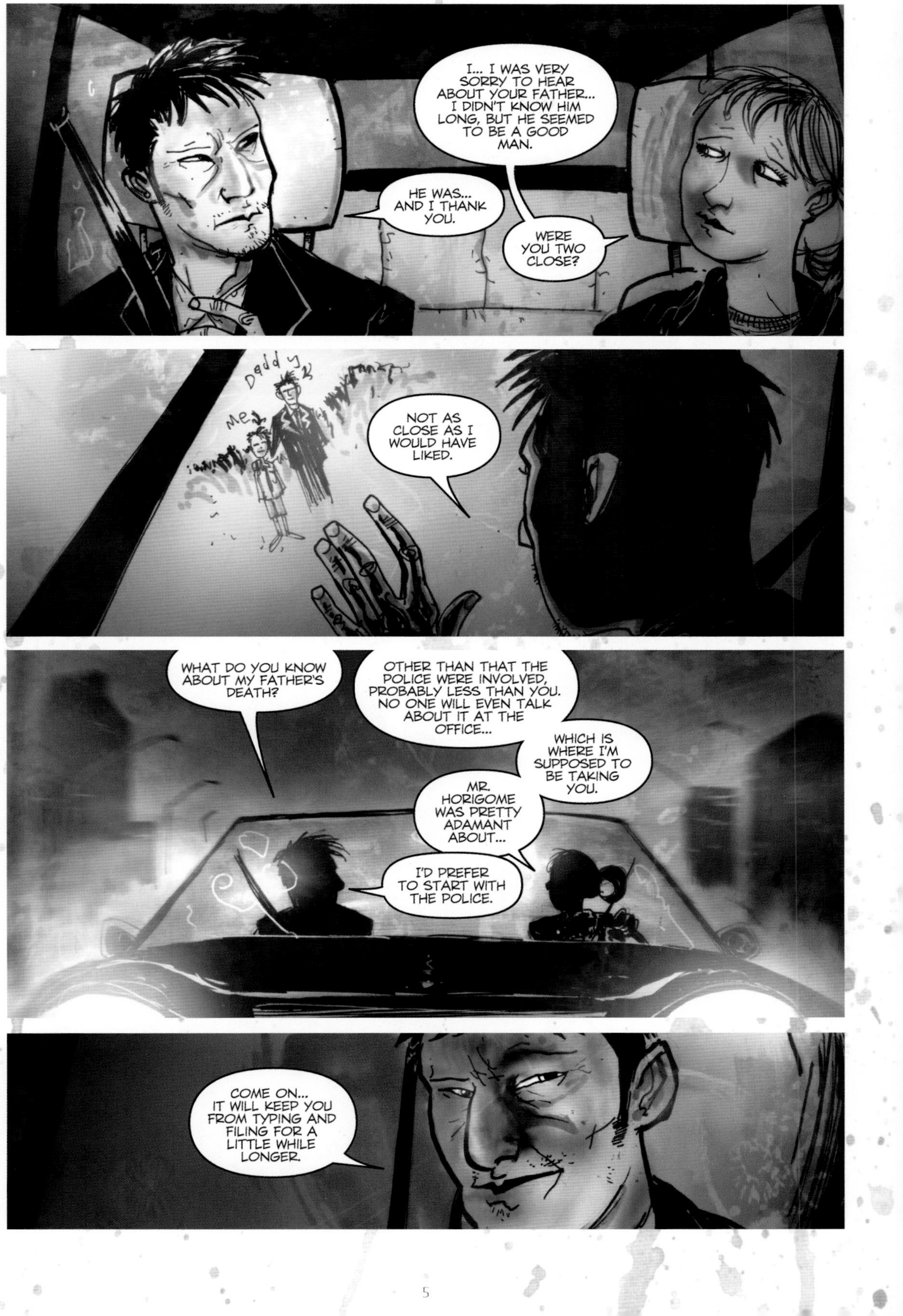
I... I WAS VERY SORRY TO HEAR ABOUT YOUR FATHER... I DIDN'T KNOW HIM LONG, BUT HE SEEMED TO BE A GOOD MAN.
HE WAS... AND I THANK YOU.
WERE YOU TWO CLOSE?
Daddy
Me
NOT AS CLOSE AS I WOULD HAVE LIKED.
WHAT DO YOU KNOW ABOUT MY FATHER'S DEATH?
OTHER THAN THAT THE POLICE WERE INVOLVED, PROBABLY LESS THAN YOU. NO ONE WILL EVEN TALK ABOUT IT AT THE OFFICE...
WHICH IS WHERE I'M SUPPOSED TO BE TAKING YOU.
MR. HORIGOME WAS PRETTY ADAMANT ABOUT...
I'D PREFER TO START WITH THE POLICE.
COME ON... IT WILL KEEP YOU FROM TYPING AND FILING FOR A LITTLE WHILE LONGER.

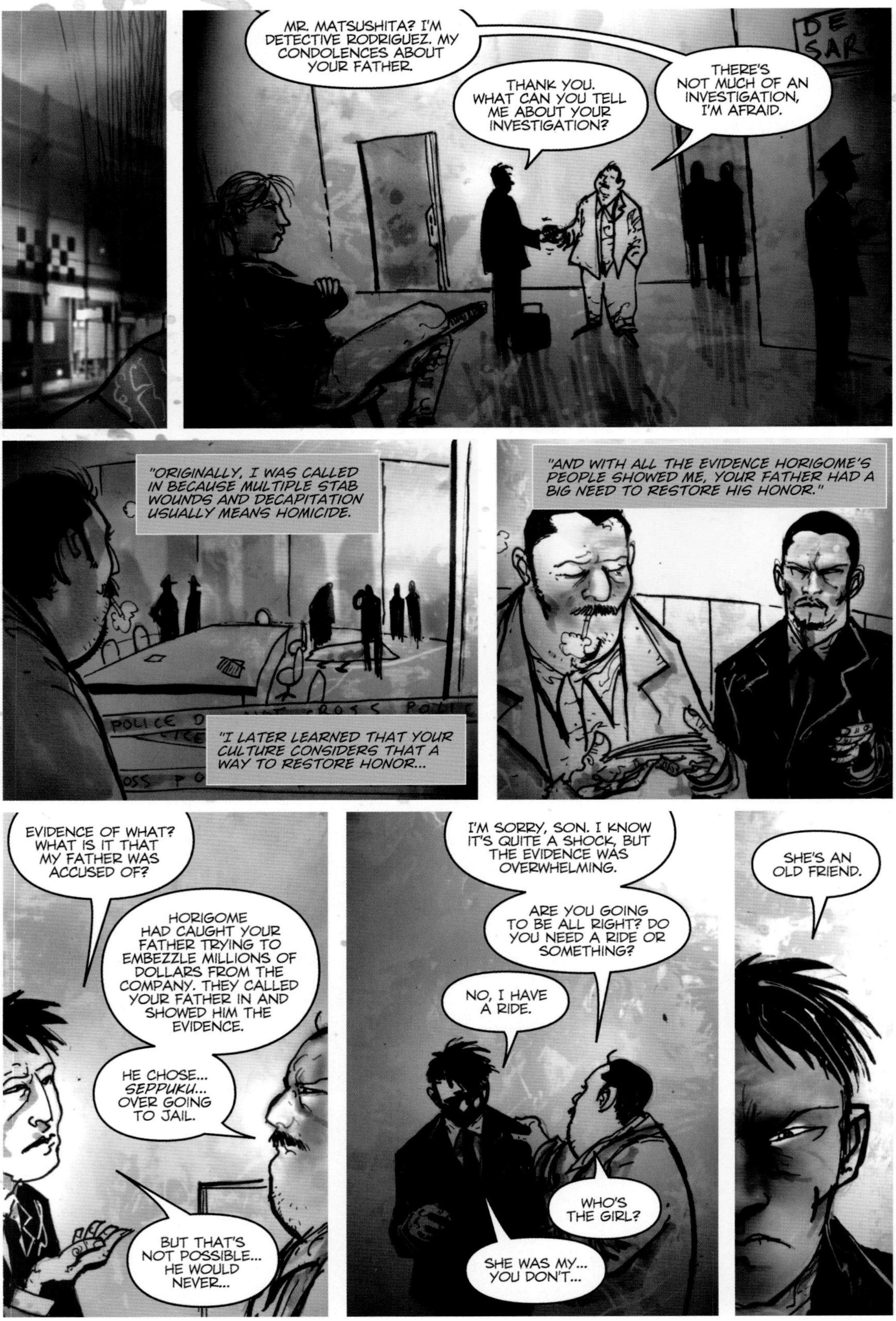

MR. MATSUSHITA? I'M DETECTIVE RODRIGUEZ. MY CONDOLENCES ABOUT YOUR FATHER.
THANK YOU. WHAT CAN YOU TELL ME ABOUT YOUR INVESTIGATION?
THERE'S NOT MUCH OF AN INVESTIGATION, I'M AFRAID.
"ORIGINALLY, I WAS CALLED IN BECAUSE MULTIPLE STAB WOUNDS AND DECAPITATION USUALLY MEANS HOMICIDE.
"I LATER LEARNED THAT YOUR CULTURE CONSIDERS THAT A WAY TO RESTORE HONOR...
"AND WITH ALL THE EVIDENCE HORIGOME'S PEOPLE SHOWED ME, YOUR FATHER HAD A BIG NEED TO RESTORE HIS HONOR."
EVIDENCE OF WHAT? WHAT IS IT THAT MY FATHER WAS ACCUSED OF?
HORIGOME HAD CAUGHT YOUR FATHER TRYING TO EMBEZZLE MILLIONS OF DOLLARS FROM THE COMPANY. THEY CALLED YOUR FATHER IN AND SHOWED HIM THE EVIDENCE.
HE CHOSE... SEPPUKU... OVER GOING TO JAIL.
BUT THAT'S NOT POSSIBLE... HE WOULD NEVER...
I'M SORRY, SON. I KNOW IT'S QUITE A SHOCK, BUT THE EVIDENCE WAS OVERWHELMING.
ARE YOU GOING TO BE ALL RIGHT? DO YOU NEED A RIDE OR SOMETHING?
NO, I HAVE A RIDE.
WHO'S THE GIRL?
SHE WAS MY... YOU DON'T...
SHE'S AN OLD FRIEND.

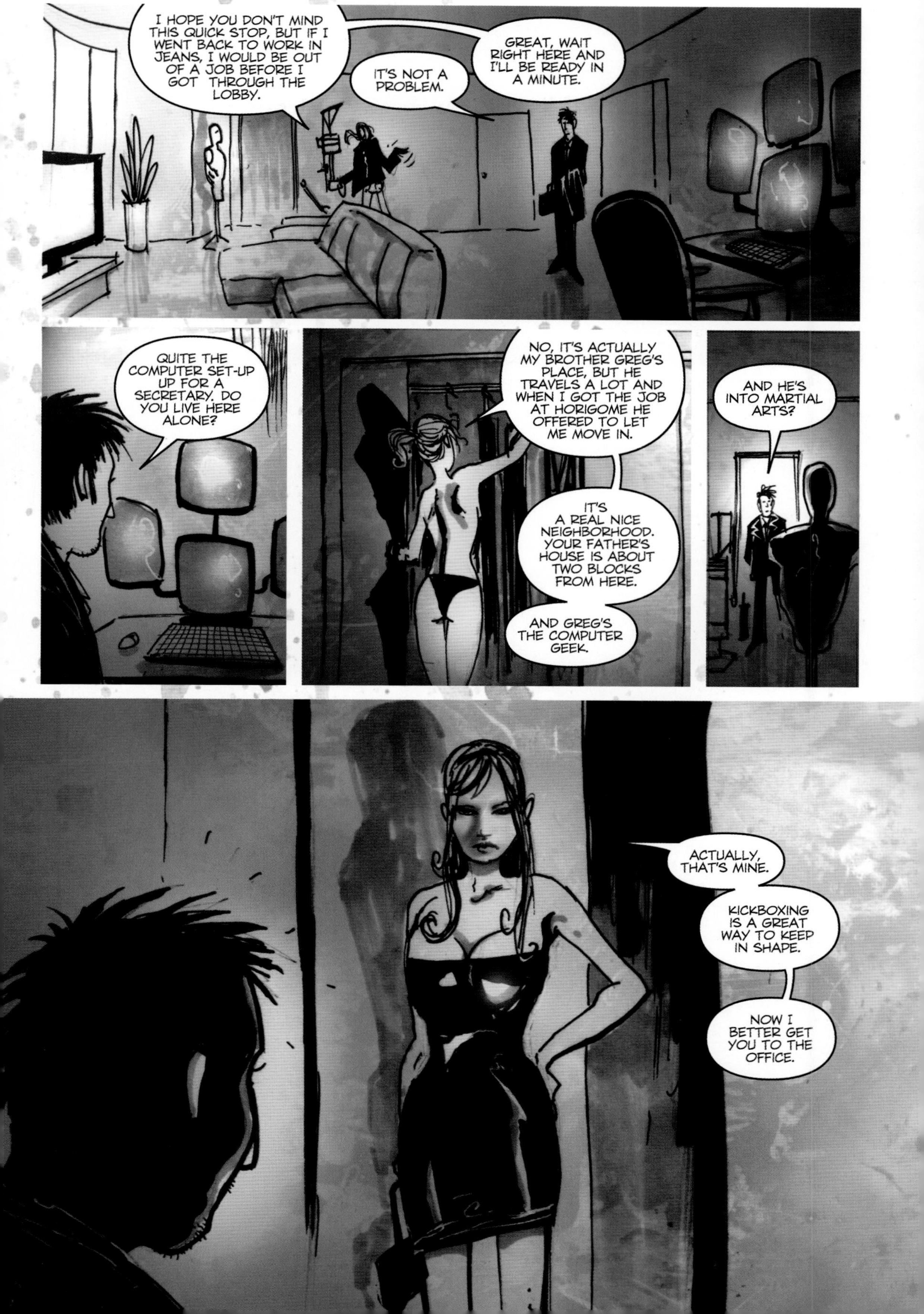
I HOPE YOU DON'T MIND THIS QUICK STOP, BUT IF I WENT BACK TO WORK IN JEANS, I WOULD BE OUT OF A JOB BEFORE I GOT THROUGH THE LOBBY.
IT'S NOT A PROBLEM.
GREAT, WAIT RIGHT HERE AND I'LL BE READY IN A MINUTE.
QUITE THE COMPUTER SET-UP FOR A SECRETARY. DO YOU LIVE HERE ALONE?
NO, IT'S ACTUALLY MY BROTHER GREG'S PLACE, BUT HE TRAVELS A LOT AND WHEN I GOT THE JOB AT HORIGOME HE OFFERED TO LET ME MOVE IN.
IT'S A REAL NICE NEIGHBORHOOD. YOUR FATHER'S HOUSE IS ABOUT TWO BLOCKS FROM HERE.
AND GREG'S THE COMPUTER GEEK.
AND HE'S INTO MARTIAL ARTS?
ACTUALLY, THAT'S MINE.
KICKBOXING IS A GREAT WAY TO KEEP IN SHAPE.
NOW I BETTER GET YOU TO THE OFFICE.

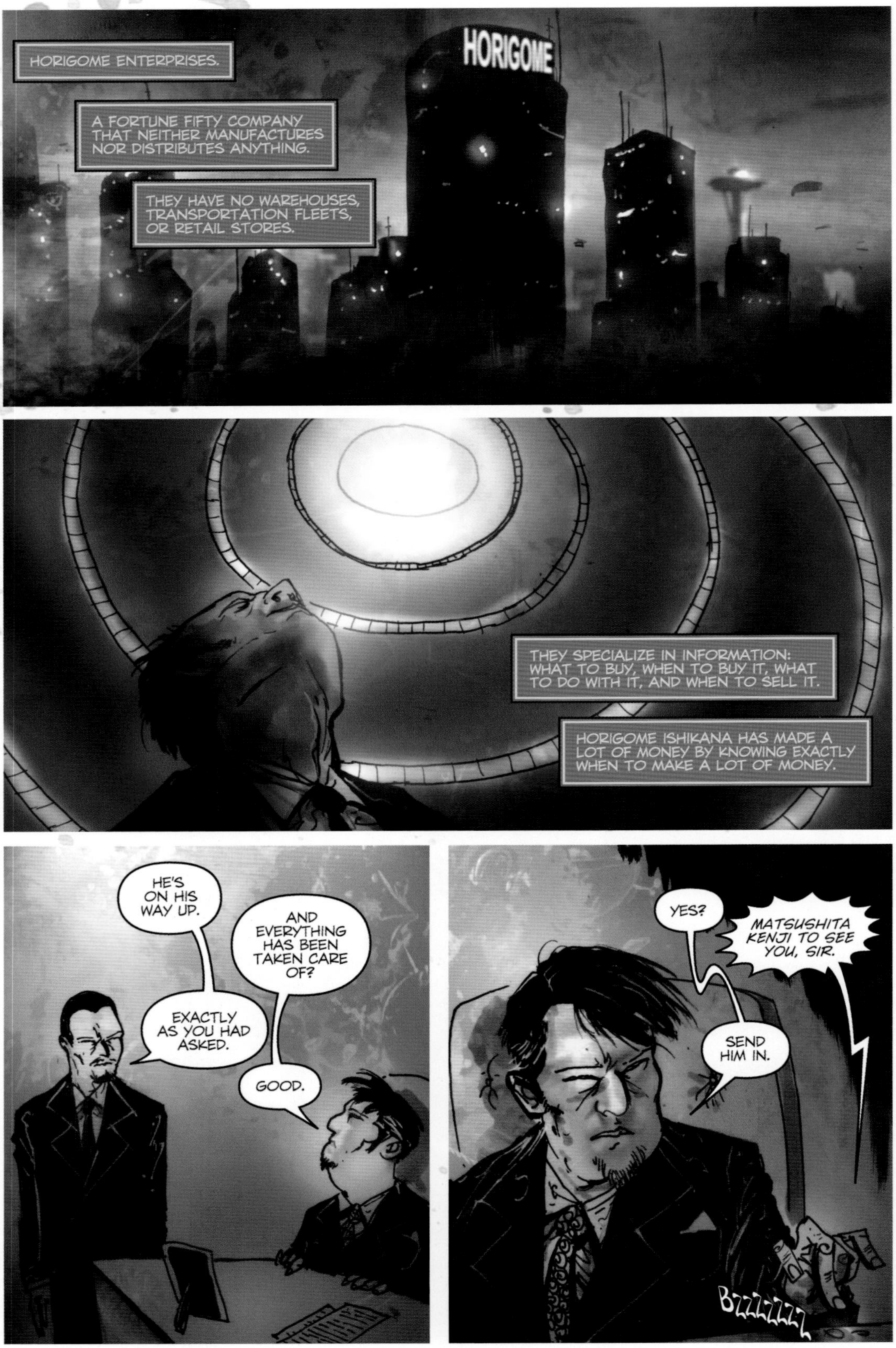
HORIGOME ENTERPRISES.
A FORTUNE FIFTY COMPANY THAT NEITHER MANUFACTURES NOR DISTRIBUTES ANYTHING.
THEY HAVE NO WAREHOUSES, TRANSPORTATION FLEETS, OR RETAIL STORES.
HORIGOME
THEY SPECIALIZE IN INFORMATION: WHAT TO BUY, WHEN TO BUY IT, WHAT TO DO WITH IT, AND WHEN TO SELL IT.
HORIGOME ISHIKANA HAS MADE A LOT OF MONEY BY KNOWING EXACTLY WHEN TO MAKE A LOT OF MONEY.
HE'S ON HIS WAY UP.
AND EVERYTHING HAS BEEN TAKEN CARE OF?
EXACTLY AS YOU HAD ASKED.
GOOD.
BZZZZZZZ
YES?
MATSUSHITA KENJI TO SEE YOU, SIR.
SEND HIM IN.

KENJI, MY BOY, IT'S BEEN FAR TOO LONG...

IF ONLY IT WERE UNDER HAPPIER CIRCUMSTANCES.

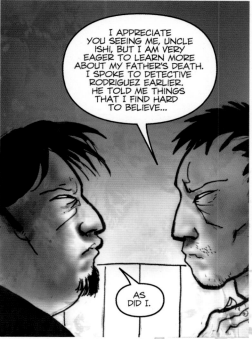

I APPRECIATE YOU SEEING ME, UNCLE ISHI, BUT I AM VERY EAGER TO LEARN MORE ABOUT MY FATHER'S DEATH. I SPOKE TO DETECTIVE RODRIGUEZ EARLIER. HE TOLD ME THINGS THAT I FIND HARD TO BELIEVE...

AS DID I.

THIS IS MY HEAD OF SECURITY, YASUNARI JIN.

HE IS THE ONE WHO DISCOVERED WHAT YOUR FATHER HAD BEEN DOING.

I WAS LOOKING INTO SOME MINOR DISCREPANCIES THAT ONE OF OUR ACCOUNTANTS BROUGHT TO MY ATTENTION. AS I FOLLOWED THE TRAIL BACK, I DISCOVERED THAT THESE DISCREPANCIES WERE CONSISTENT OVER THE LAST EIGHTEEN MONTHS... AND THEY ALL CAME FROM YOUR FATHER'S OFFICE.

WHEN JIN BROUGHT IT TO MY ATTENTION, I TOLD HIM I WISHED TO HANDLE THIS INTERNALLY. HE WAS TO TAKE THE EVIDENCE TO YOUR FATHER AND ALLOW HIM TO EXPLAIN.

YOUR FATHER REALIZED THAT HE HAD BEEN CAUGHT AND CHOSE TO END HIS OWN LIFE RATHER THAN DISHONOR HIS FAMILY NAME.

HE ASKED ME TO BE HIS SECOND. I CAN TELL YOU HIS PASSING WAS QUICK... AND HONORABLE.

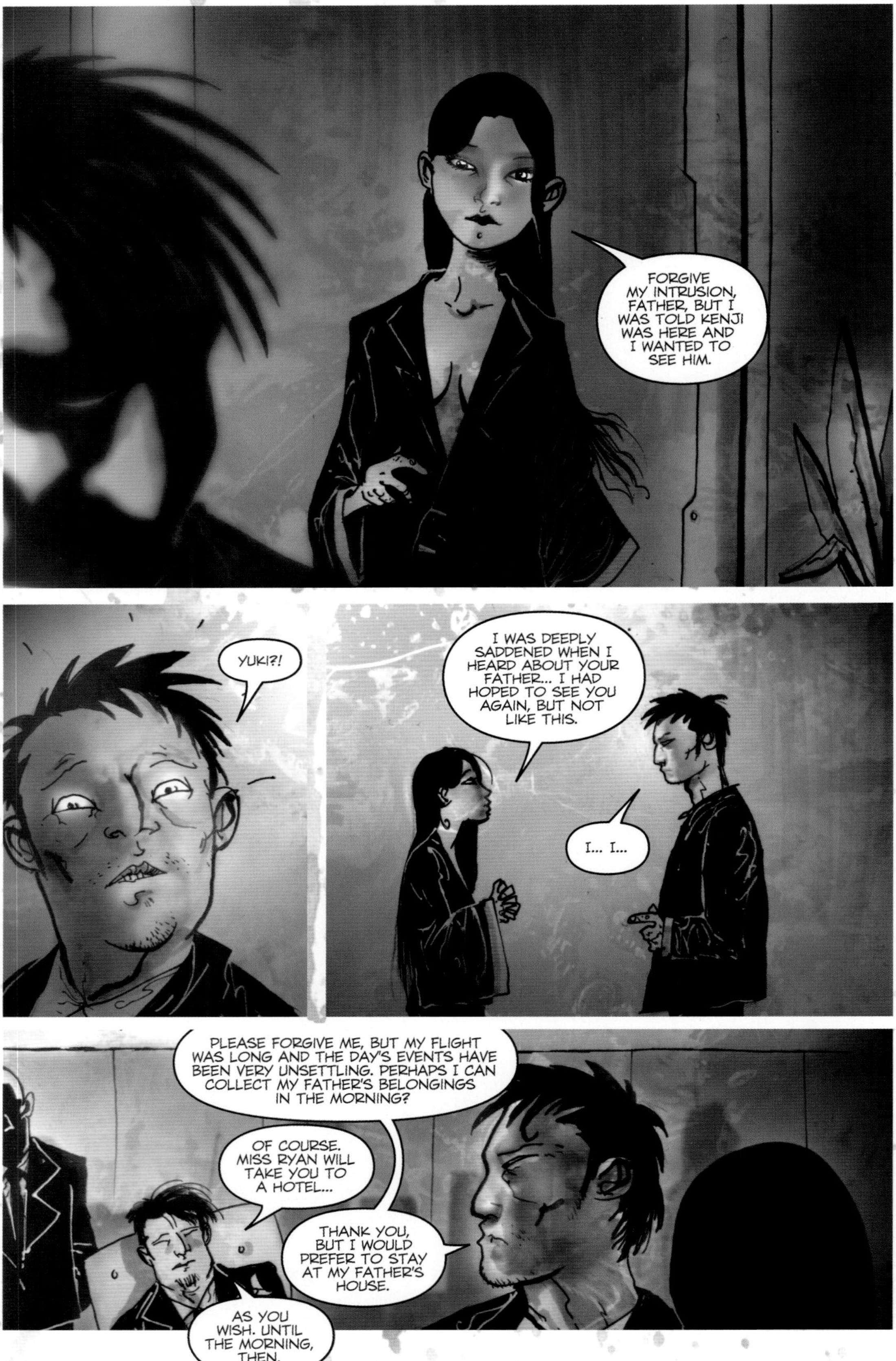
FORGIVE MY INTRUSION, FATHER, BUT I WAS TOLD KENJI WAS HERE AND I WANTED TO SEE HIM.
YUKI?!
I WAS DEEPLY SADDENED WHEN I HEARD ABOUT YOUR FATHER... I HAD HOPED TO SEE YOU AGAIN, BUT NOT LIKE THIS.
I... I...
PLEASE FORGIVE ME, BUT MY FLIGHT WAS LONG AND THE DAY'S EVENTS HAVE BEEN VERY UNSETTLING. PERHAPS I CAN COLLECT MY FATHER'S BELONGINGS IN THE MORNING?
OF COURSE. MISS RYAN WILL TAKE YOU TO A HOTEL...
THANK YOU, BUT I WOULD PREFER TO STAY AT MY FATHER'S HOUSE.
AS YOU WISH. UNTIL THE MORNING, THEN.

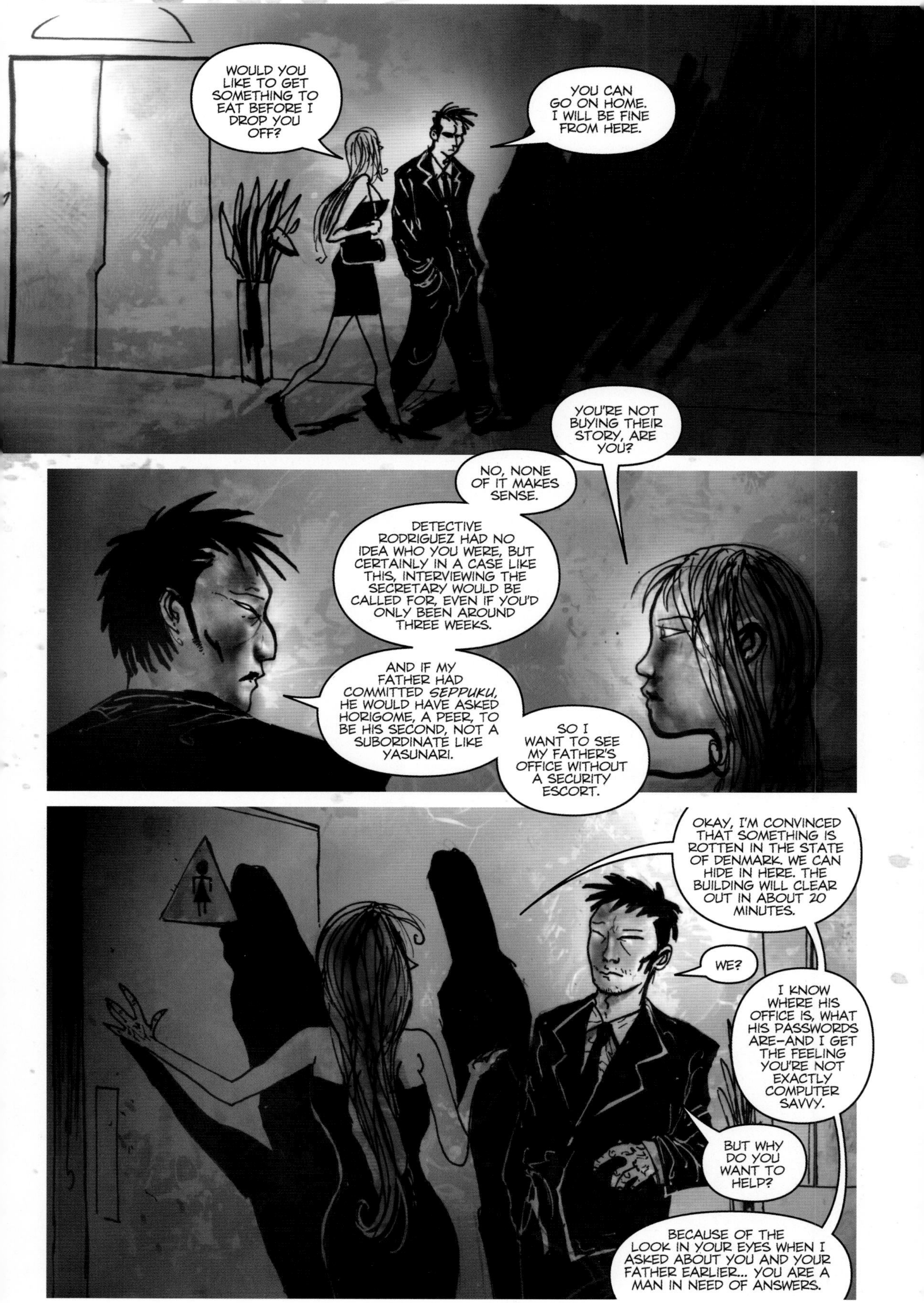

WOULD YOU LIKE TO GET SOMETHING TO EAT BEFORE I DROP YOU OFF?
YOU CAN GO ON HOME. I WILL BE FINE FROM HERE.
YOU'RE NOT BUYING THEIR STORY, ARE YOU?
NO, NONE OF IT MAKES SENSE.
DETECTIVE RODRIGUEZ HAD NO IDEA WHO YOU WERE, BUT CERTAINLY IN A CASE LIKE THIS, INTERVIEWING THE SECRETARY WOULD BE CALLED FOR, EVEN IF YOU'D ONLY BEEN AROUND THREE WEEKS.
AND IF MY FATHER HAD COMMITTED *SEPPUKU*, HE WOULD HAVE ASKED HORIGOME, A PEER, TO BE HIS SECOND, NOT A SUBORDINATE LIKE YASUNARI.
SO I WANT TO SEE MY FATHER'S OFFICE WITHOUT A SECURITY ESCORT.
OKAY, I'M CONVINCED THAT SOMETHING IS ROTTEN IN THE STATE OF DENMARK. WE CAN HIDE IN HERE. THE BUILDING WILL CLEAR OUT IN ABOUT 20 MINUTES.
WE?
I KNOW WHERE HIS OFFICE IS, WHAT HIS PASSWORDS ARE–AND I GET THE FEELING YOU'RE NOT EXACTLY COMPUTER SAVVY.
BUT WHY DO YOU WANT TO HELP?
BECAUSE OF THE LOOK IN YOUR EYES WHEN I ASKED ABOUT YOU AND YOUR FATHER EARLIER... YOU ARE A MAN IN NEED OF ANSWERS.

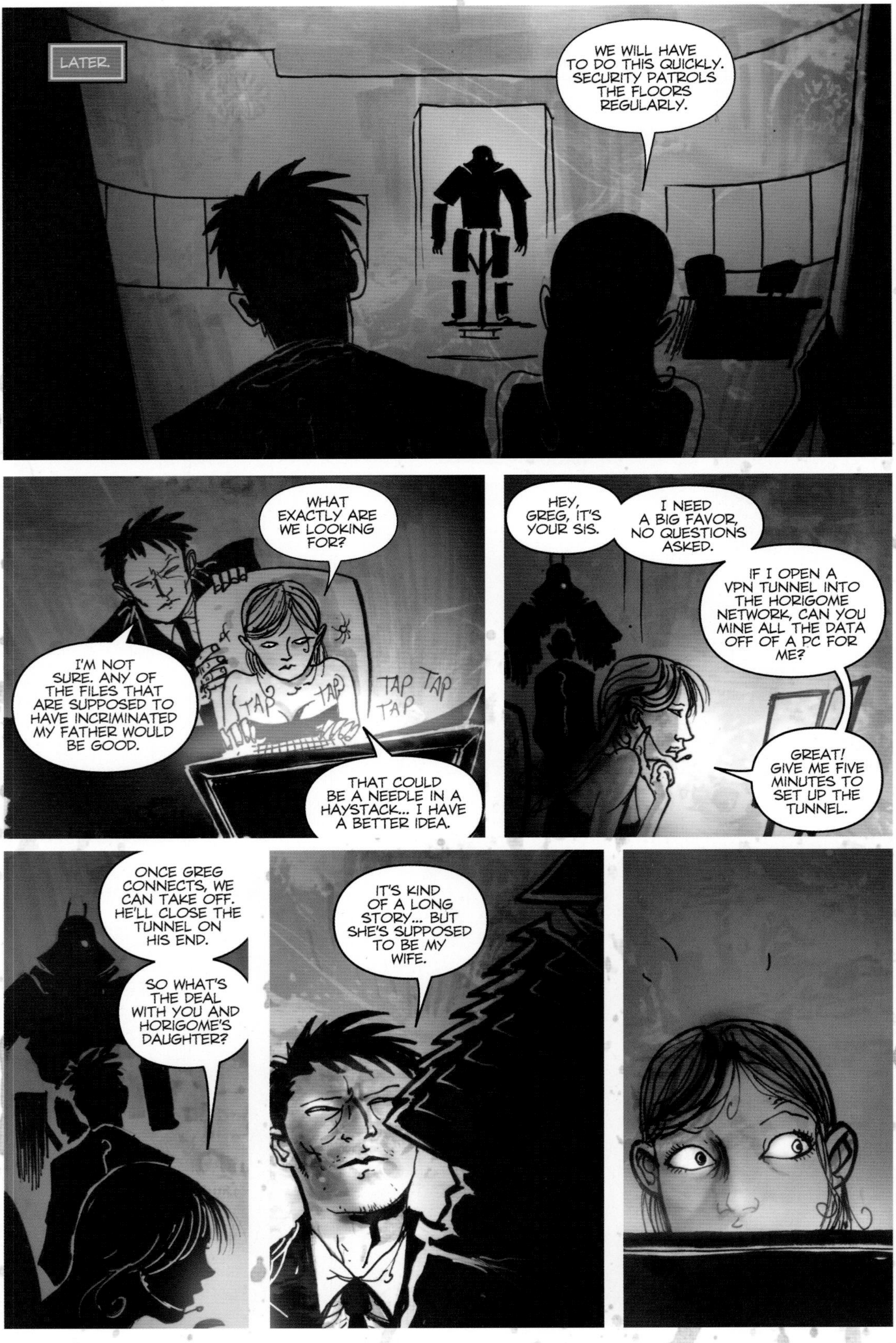
LATER.
WE WILL HAVE TO DO THIS QUICKLY. SECURITY PATROLS THE FLOORS REGULARLY.
WHAT EXACTLY ARE WE LOOKING FOR?
I'M NOT SURE. ANY OF THE FILES THAT ARE SUPPOSED TO HAVE INCRIMINATED MY FATHER WOULD BE GOOD.
TAP TAP TAP TAP TAP
THAT COULD BE A NEEDLE IN A HAYSTACK... I HAVE A BETTER IDEA.
HEY, GREG, IT'S YOUR SIS.
I NEED A BIG FAVOR, NO QUESTIONS ASKED.
IF I OPEN A VPN TUNNEL INTO THE HORIGOME NETWORK, CAN YOU MINE ALL THE DATA OFF OF A PC FOR ME?
GREAT! GIVE ME FIVE MINUTES TO SET UP THE TUNNEL.
ONCE GREG CONNECTS, WE CAN TAKE OFF. HE'LL CLOSE THE TUNNEL ON HIS END.
SO WHAT'S THE DEAL WITH YOU AND HORIGOME'S DAUGHTER?
IT'S KIND OF A LONG STORY... BUT SHE'S SUPPOSED TO BE MY WIFE.

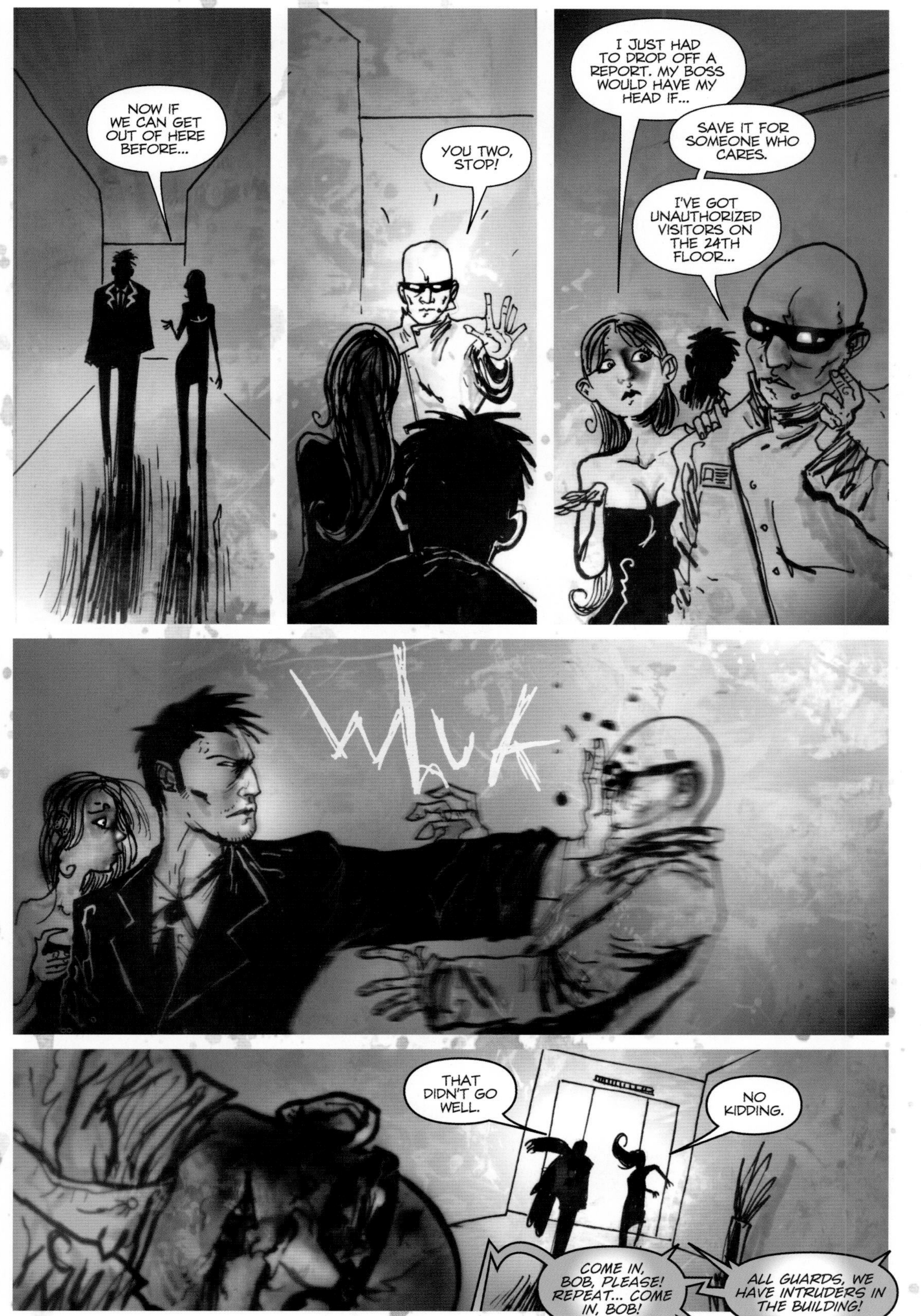
NOW IF WE CAN GET OUT OF HERE BEFORE...
YOU TWO, STOP!
I JUST HAD TO DROP OFF A REPORT. MY BOSS WOULD HAVE MY HEAD IF...
SAVE IT FOR SOMEONE WHO CARES.
I'VE GOT UNAUTHORIZED VISITORS ON THE 24TH FLOOR...
THAT DIDN'T GO WELL.
NO KIDDING.
COME IN, BOB, PLEASE! REPEAT... COME IN, BOB!
ALL GUARDS, WE HAVE INTRUDERS IN THE BUILDING!

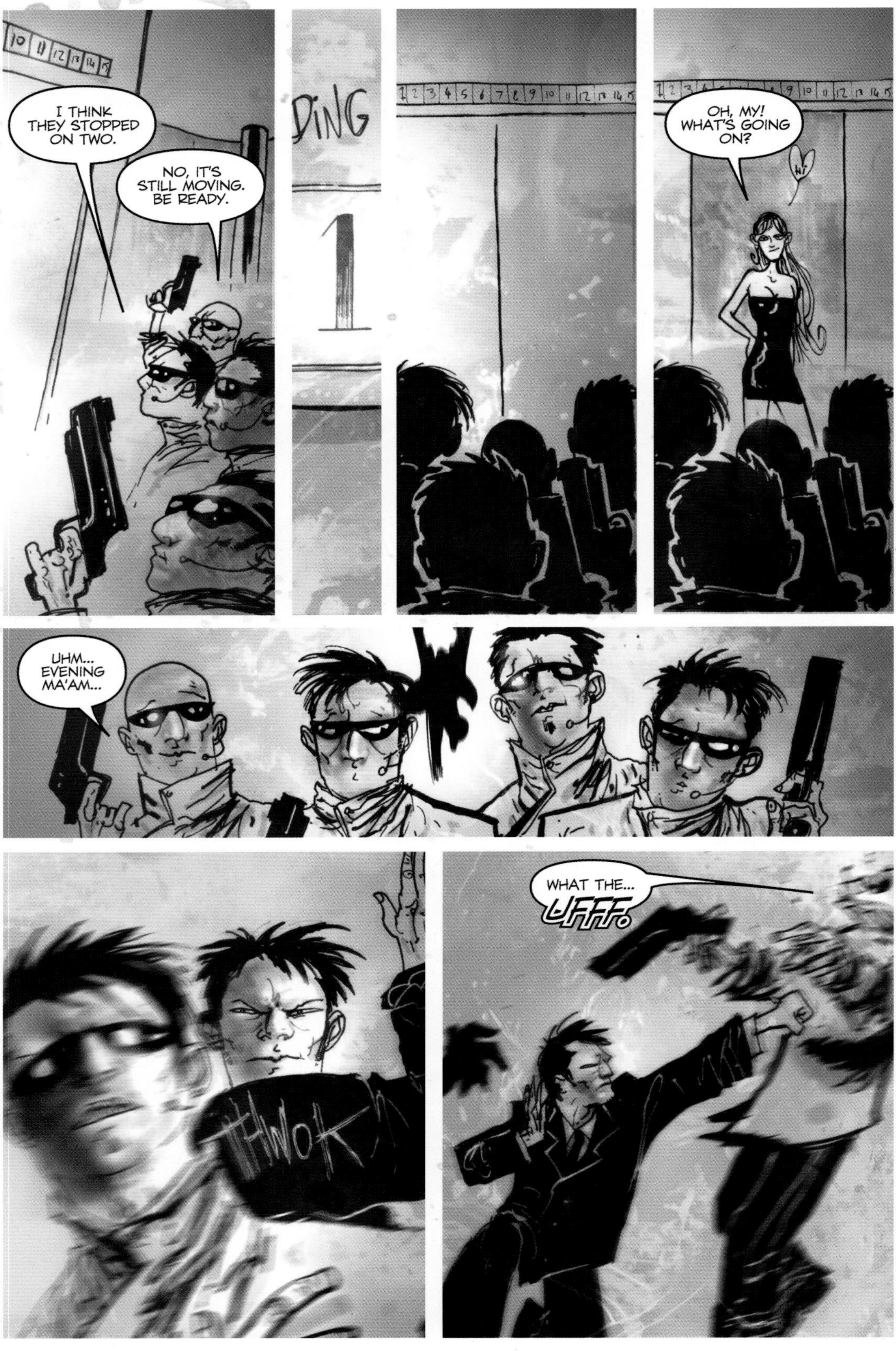
I THINK THEY STOPPED ON TWO.
NO, IT'S STILL MOVING. BE READY.
DING
1
OH, MY! WHAT'S GOING ON?
UHM... EVENING MA'AM...
THWOK
WHAT THE... UFFF.

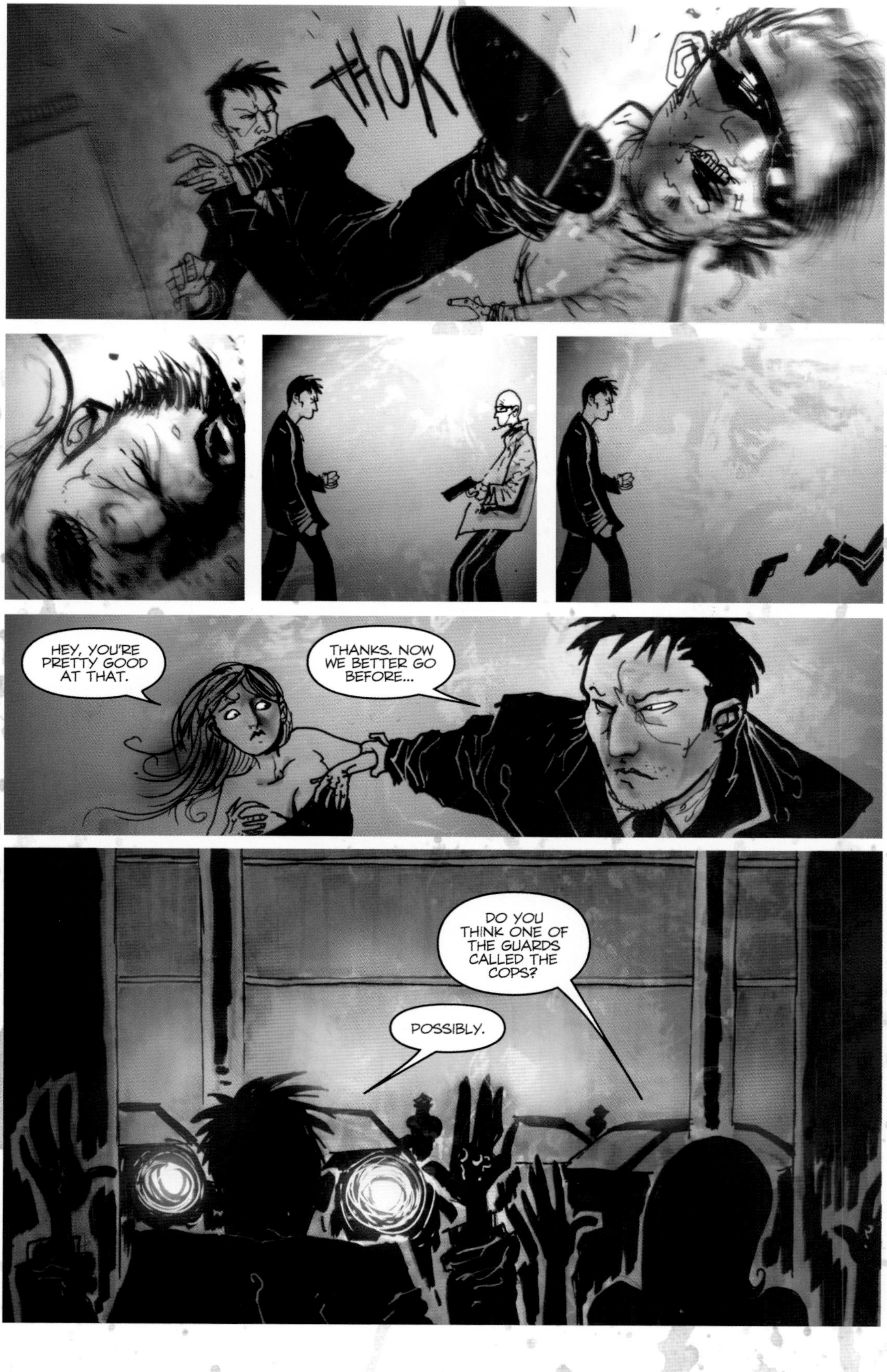
THOK
HEY, YOU'RE PRETTY GOOD AT THAT.
THANKS. NOW WE BETTER GO BEFORE...
DO YOU THINK ONE OF THE GUARDS CALLED THE COPS?
POSSIBLY.

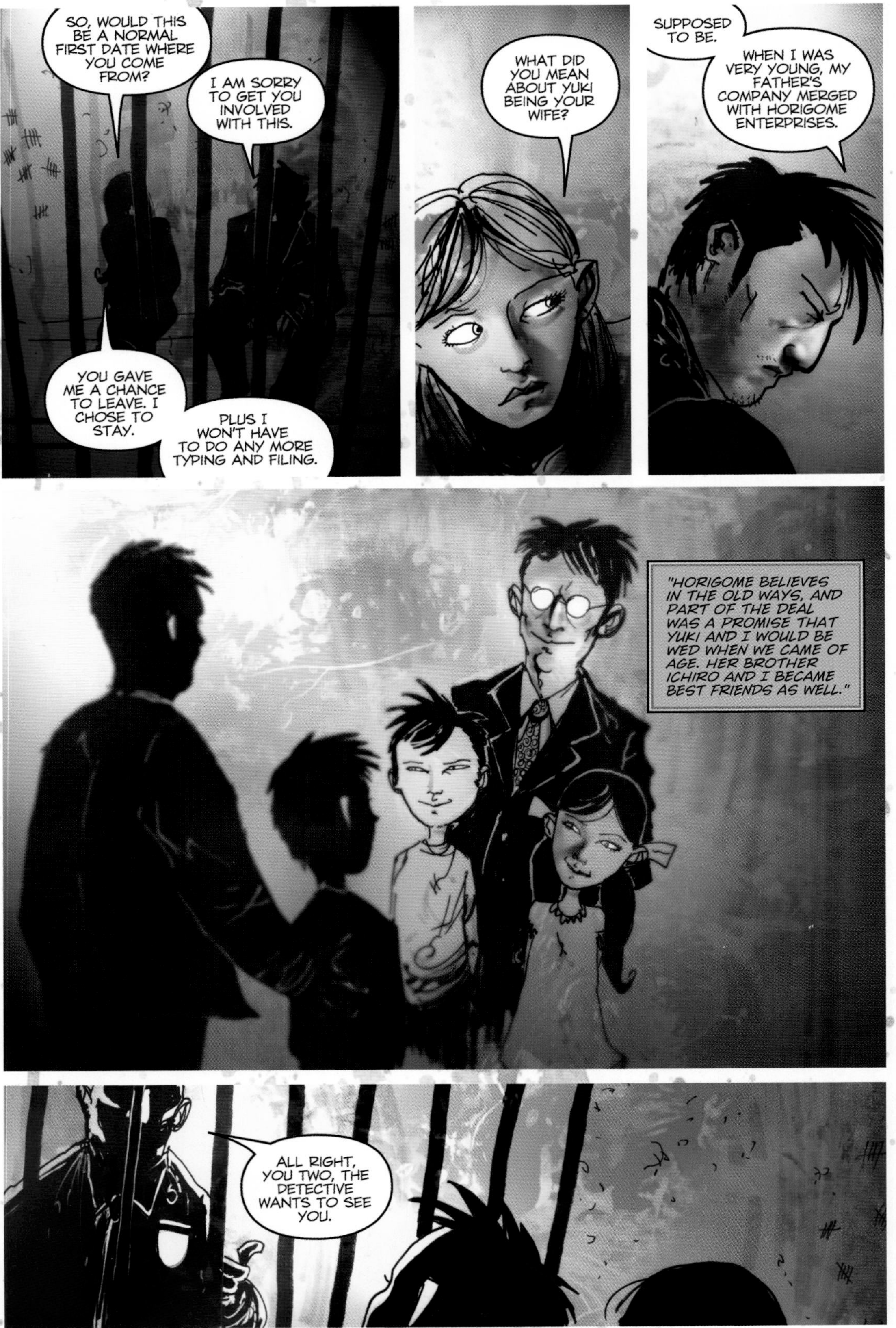
SO, WOULD THIS BE A NORMAL FIRST DATE WHERE YOU COME FROM?
I AM SORRY TO GET YOU INVOLVED WITH THIS.
YOU GAVE ME A CHANCE TO LEAVE. I CHOSE TO STAY.
PLUS I WON'T HAVE TO DO ANY MORE TYPING AND FILING.
WHAT DID YOU MEAN ABOUT YUKI BEING YOUR WIFE?
SUPPOSED TO BE.
WHEN I WAS VERY YOUNG, MY FATHER'S COMPANY MERGED WITH HORIGOME ENTERPRISES.
"HORIGOME BELIEVES IN THE OLD WAYS, AND PART OF THE DEAL WAS A PROMISE THAT YUKI AND I WOULD BE WED WHEN WE CAME OF AGE. HER BROTHER ICHIRO AND I BECAME BEST FRIENDS AS WELL."
ALL RIGHT, YOU TWO, THE DETECTIVE WANTS TO SEE YOU.

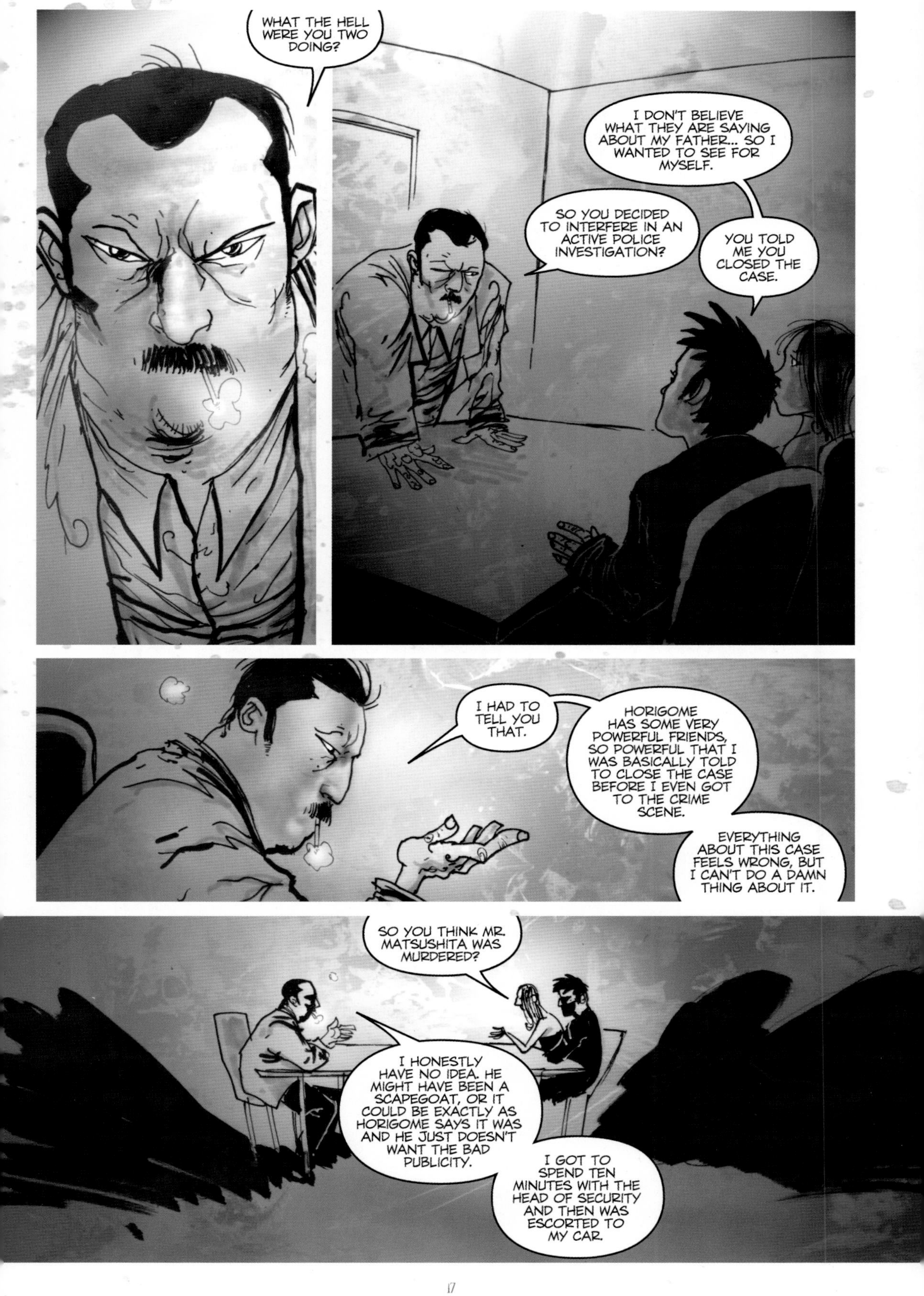
WHAT THE HELL WERE YOU TWO DOING?
I DON'T BELIEVE WHAT THEY ARE SAYING ABOUT MY FATHER... SO I WANTED TO SEE FOR MYSELF.
SO YOU DECIDED TO INTERFERE IN AN ACTIVE POLICE INVESTIGATION?
YOU TOLD ME YOU CLOSED THE CASE.
I HAD TO TELL YOU THAT.
HORIGOME HAS SOME VERY POWERFUL FRIENDS, SO POWERFUL THAT I WAS BASICALLY TOLD TO CLOSE THE CASE BEFORE I EVEN GOT TO THE CRIME SCENE.
EVERYTHING ABOUT THIS CASE FEELS WRONG, BUT I CAN'T DO A DAMN THING ABOUT IT.
SO YOU THINK MR. MATSUSHITA WAS MURDERED?
I HONESTLY HAVE NO IDEA. HE MIGHT HAVE BEEN A SCAPEGOAT, OR IT COULD BE EXACTLY AS HORIGOME SAYS IT WAS AND HE JUST DOESN'T WANT THE BAD PUBLICITY.
I GOT TO SPEND TEN MINUTES WITH THE HEAD OF SECURITY AND THEN WAS ESCORTED TO MY CAR.

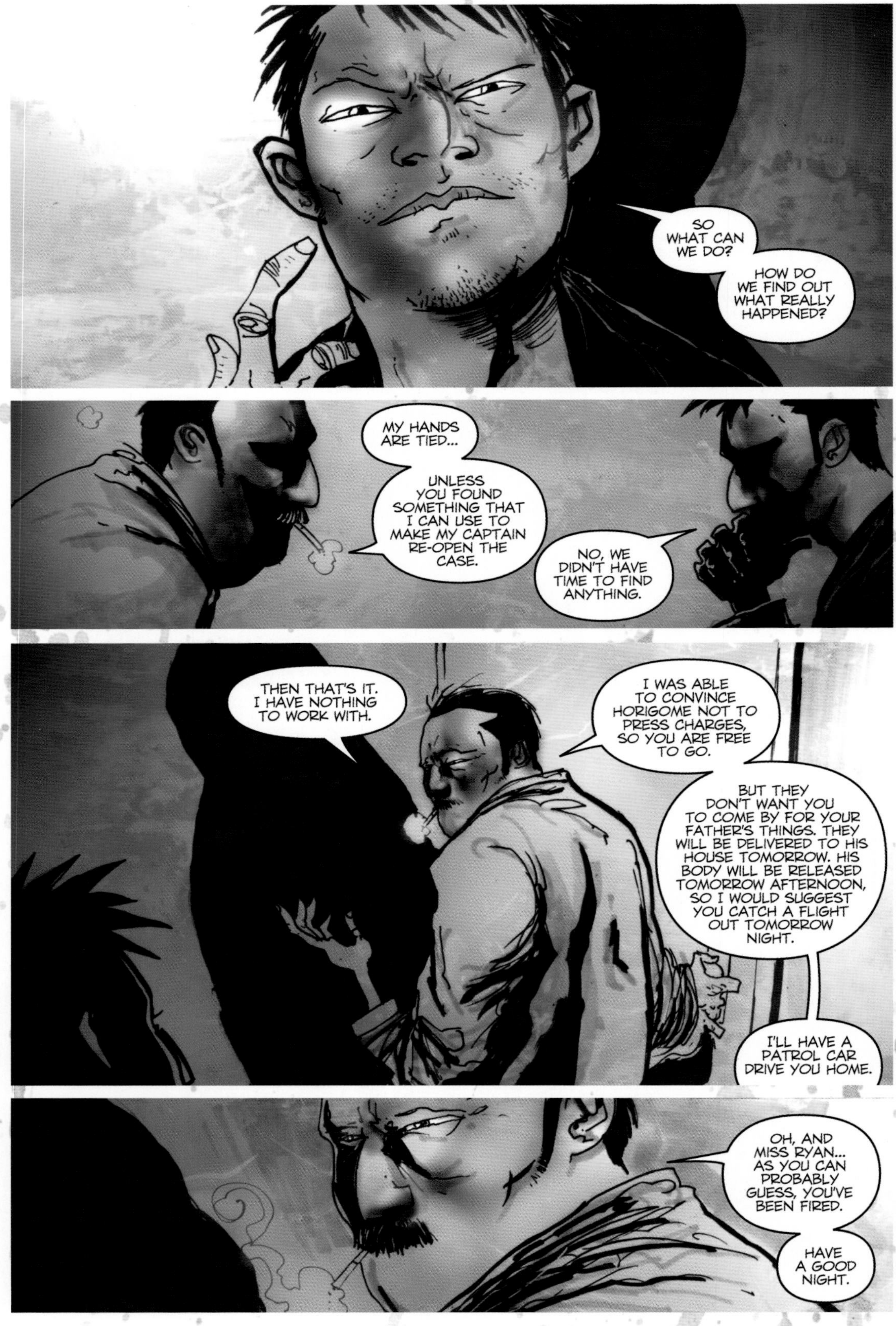
SO WHAT CAN WE DO?
HOW DO WE FIND OUT WHAT REALLY HAPPENED?
MY HANDS ARE TIED...
UNLESS YOU FOUND SOMETHING THAT I CAN USE TO MAKE MY CAPTAIN RE-OPEN THE CASE.
NO, WE DIDN'T HAVE TIME TO FIND ANYTHING.
THEN THAT'S IT. I HAVE NOTHING TO WORK WITH.
I WAS ABLE TO CONVINCE HORIGOME NOT TO PRESS CHARGES, SO YOU ARE FREE TO GO.
BUT THEY DON'T WANT YOU TO COME BY FOR YOUR FATHER'S THINGS. THEY WILL BE DELIVERED TO HIS HOUSE TOMORROW. HIS BODY WILL BE RELEASED TOMORROW AFTERNOON, SO I WOULD SUGGEST YOU CATCH A FLIGHT OUT TOMORROW NIGHT.
I'LL HAVE A PATROL CAR DRIVE YOU HOME.
OH, AND MISS RYAN... AS YOU CAN PROBABLY GUESS, YOU'VE BEEN FIRED.
HAVE A GOOD NIGHT.

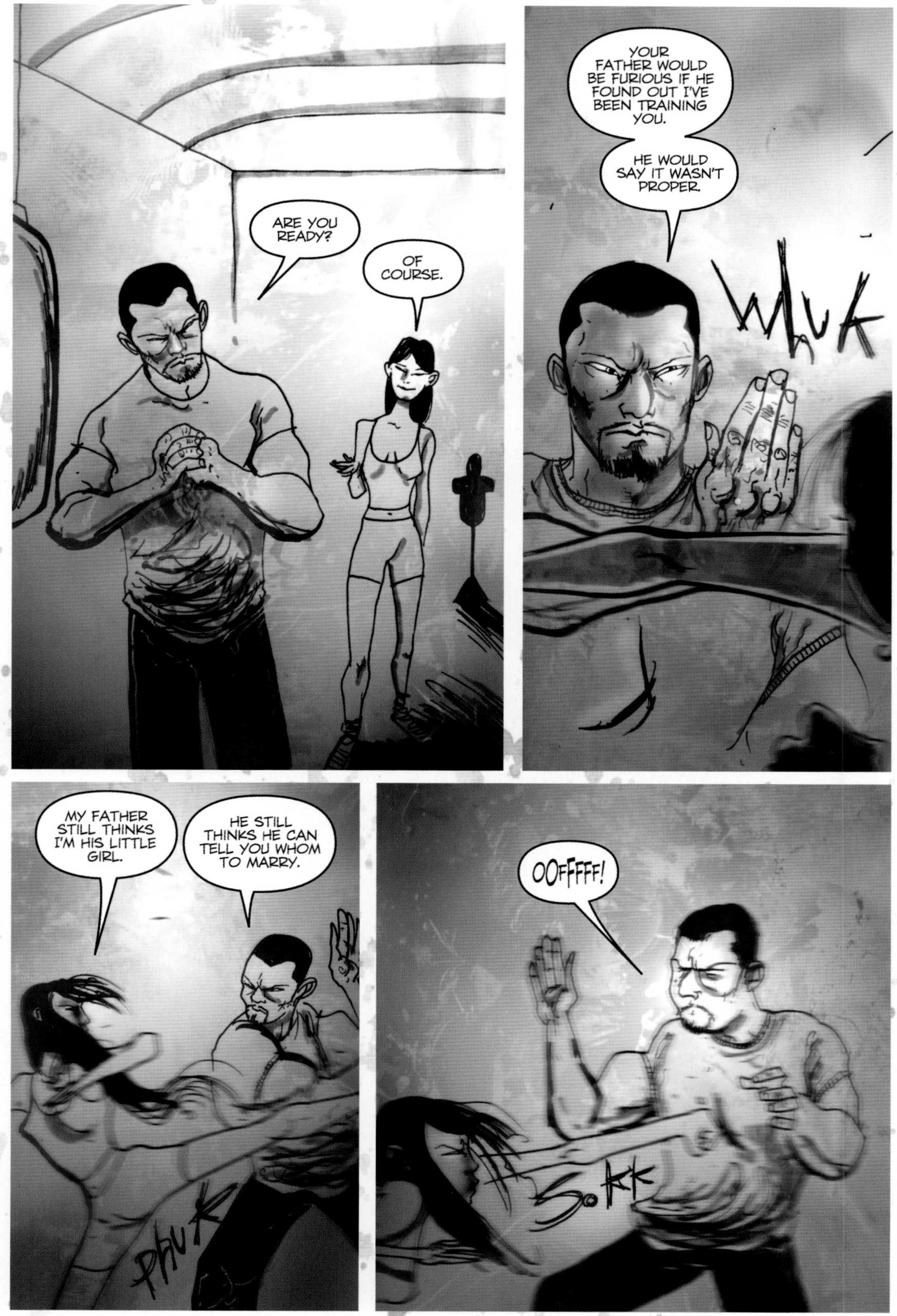
ARE YOU READY?
OF COURSE.
YOUR FATHER WOULD BE FURIOUS IF HE FOUND OUT I'VE BEEN TRAINING YOU.
HE WOULD SAY IT WASN'T PROPER.
WHUK
MY FATHER STILL THINKS I'M HIS LITTLE GIRL.
HE STILL THINKS HE CAN TELL YOU WHOM TO MARRY.
PHUK
OOFFFFF!
SOKK

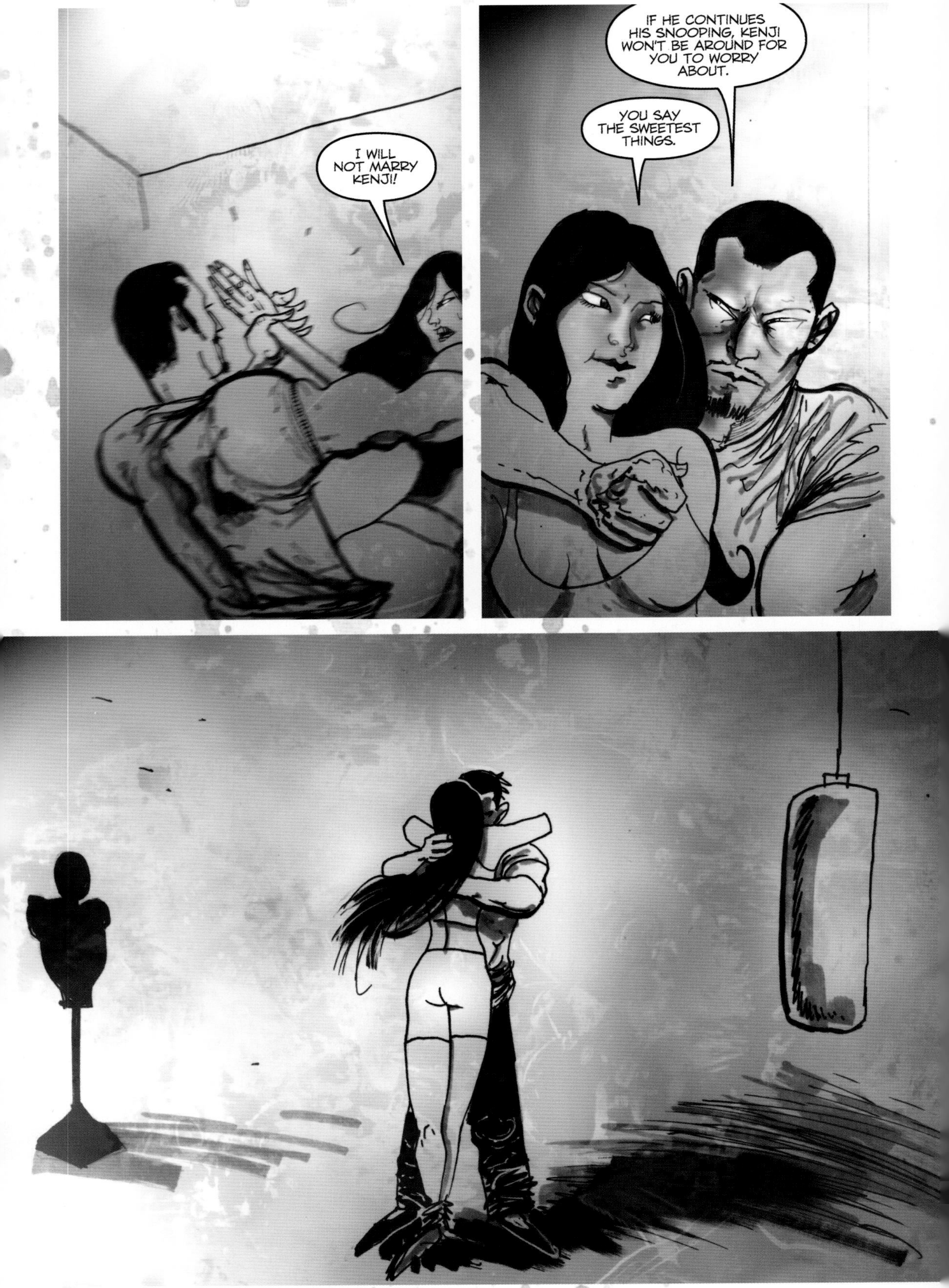
I WILL NOT MARRY KENJI!
IF HE CONTINUES HIS SNOOPING, KENJI WON'T BE AROUND FOR YOU TO WORRY ABOUT.
YOU SAY THE SWEETEST THINGS.

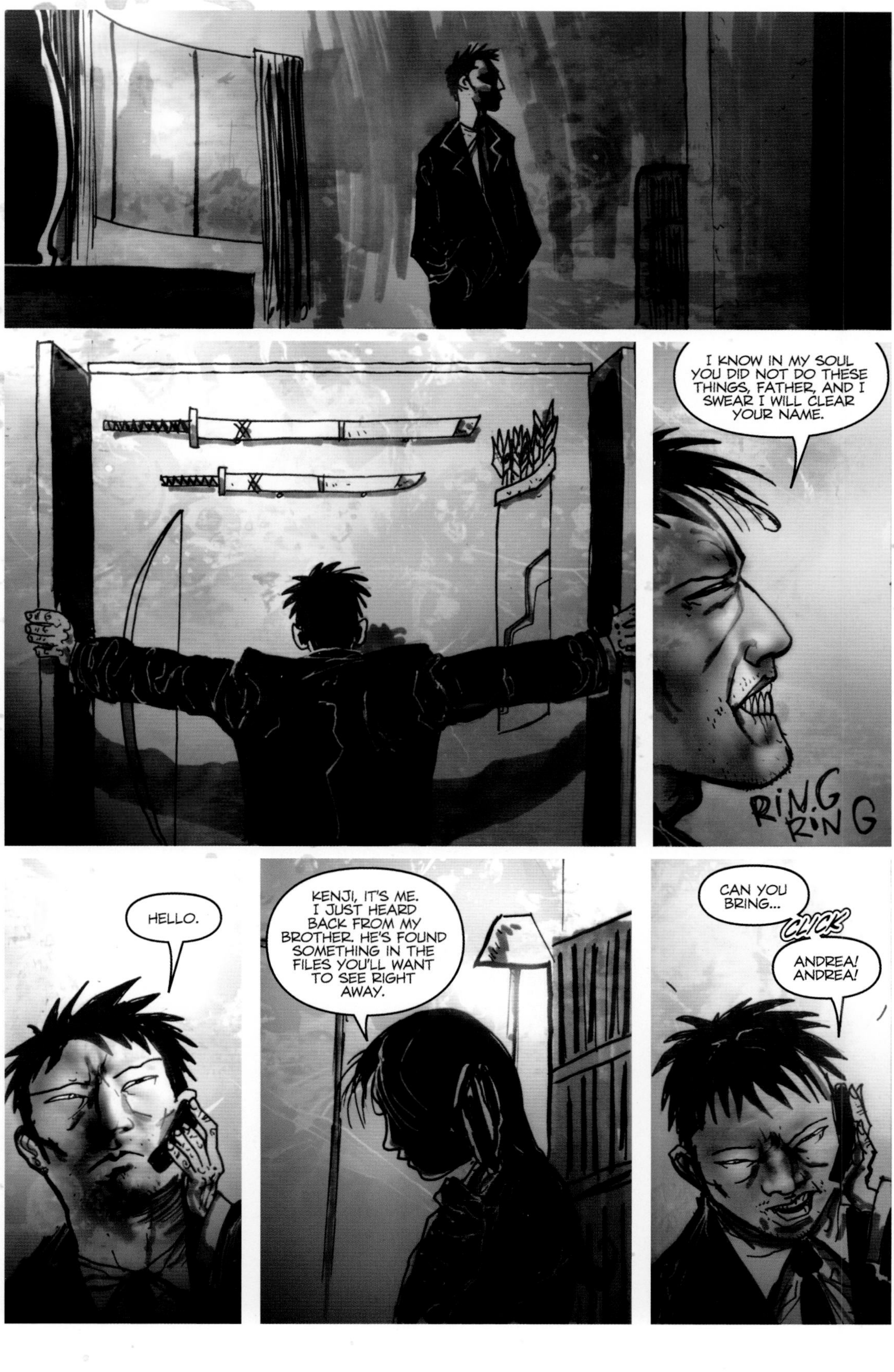
I KNOW IN MY SOUL YOU DID NOT DO THESE THINGS, FATHER, AND I SWEAR I WILL CLEAR YOUR NAME.
RING RING
HELLO.
KENJI, IT'S ME. I JUST HEARD BACK FROM MY BROTHER. HE'S FOUND SOMETHING IN THE FILES YOU'LL WANT TO SEE RIGHT AWAY.
CAN YOU BRING...
CLICK
ANDREA! ANDREA!

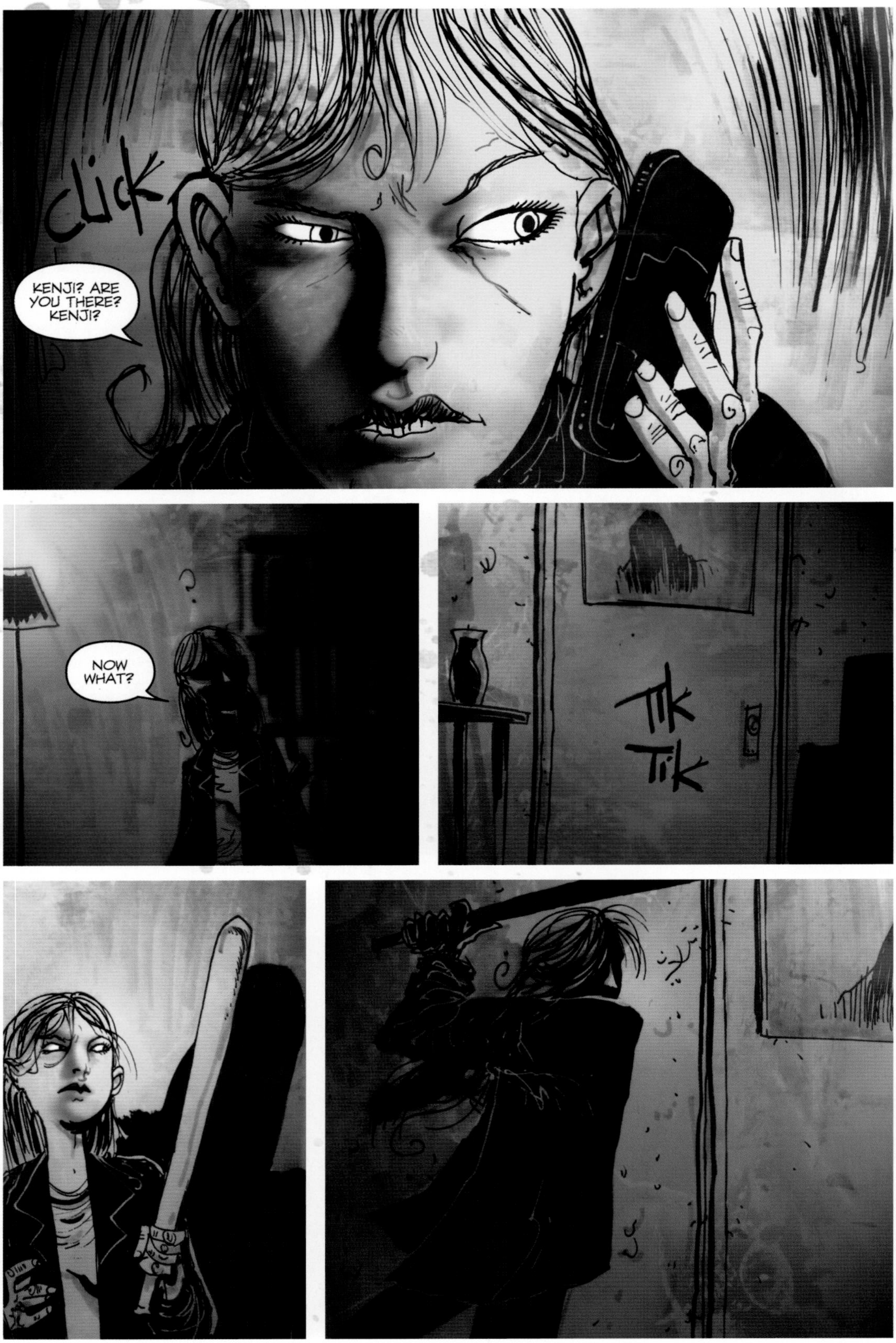
CLICK
KENJI? ARE YOU THERE? KENJI?
NOW WHAT?
TIK
TIK

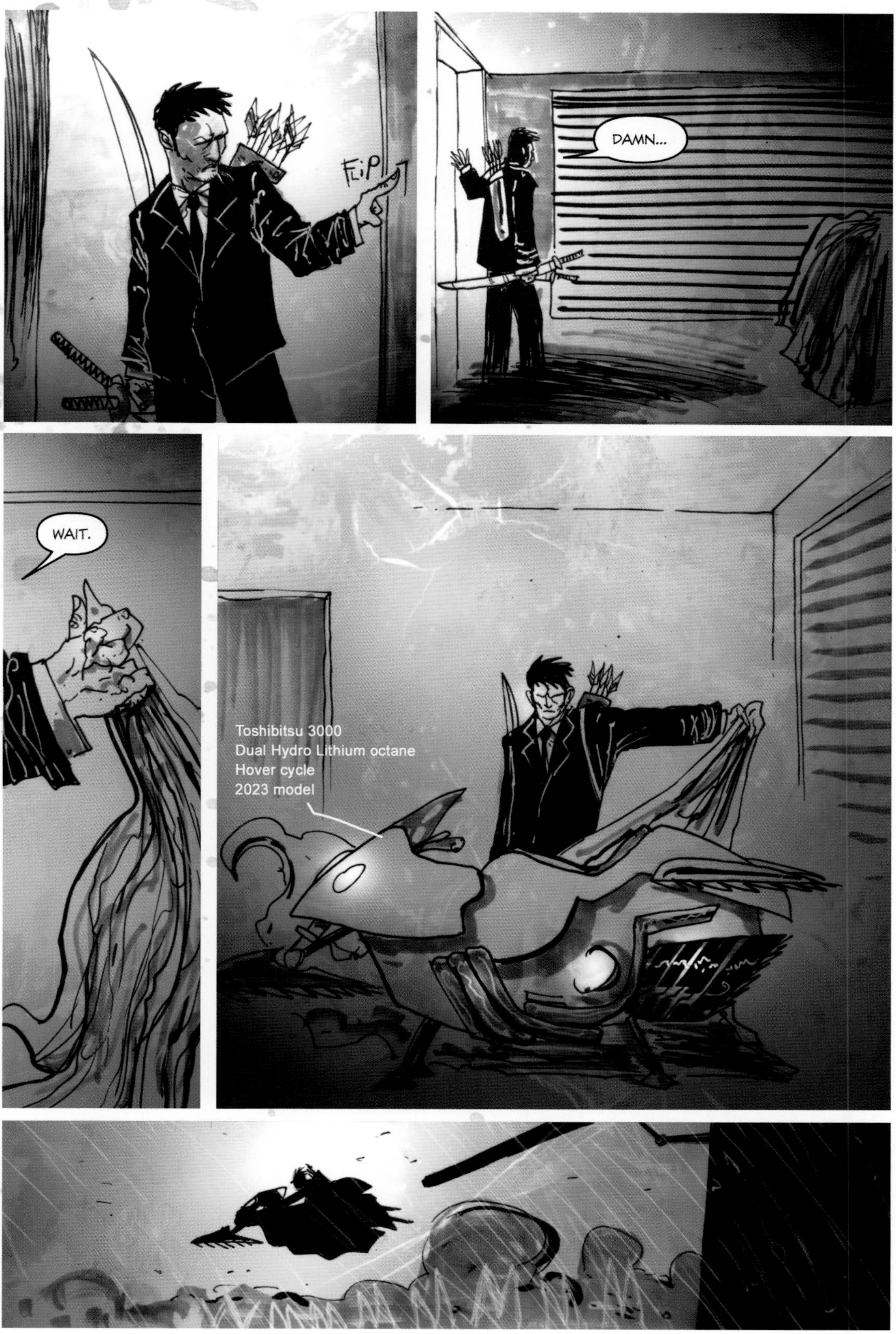
FLIP
DAMN...
WAIT.
Toshibitsu 3000
Dual Hydro Lithium octane
Hover cycle
2023 model

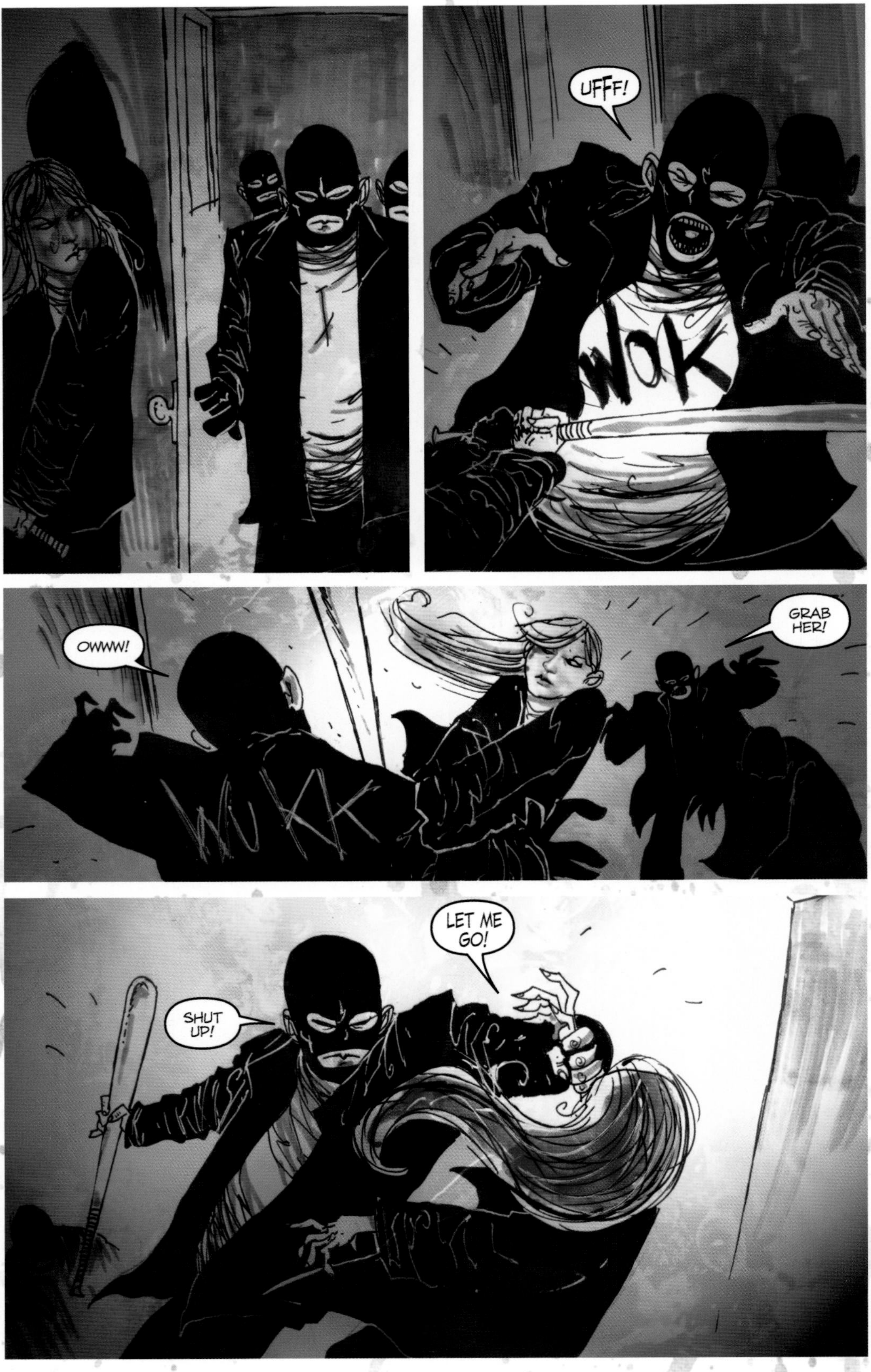
UFFF!
WOK
OWWW!
GRAB HER!
LET ME GO!
SHUT UP!

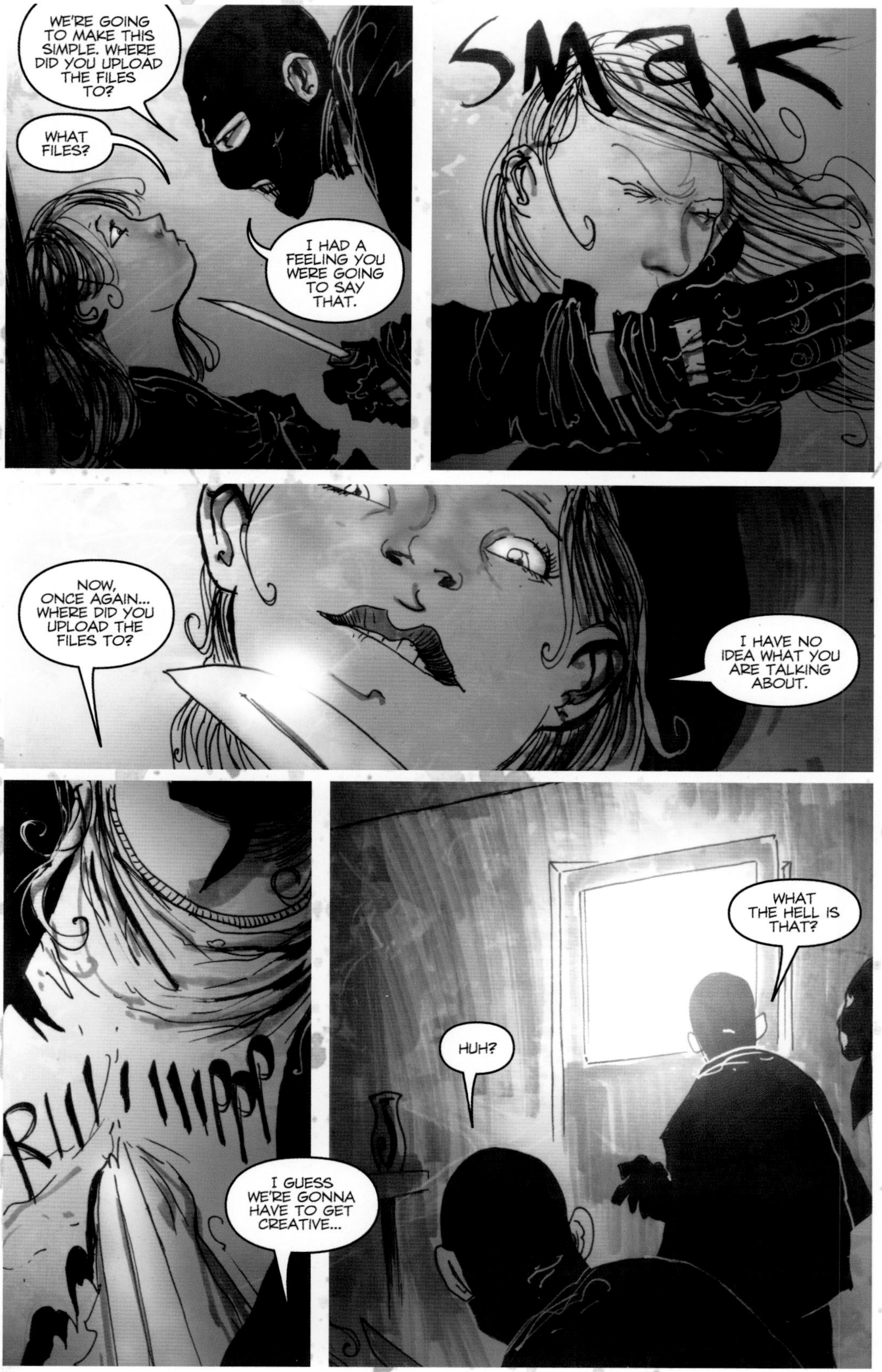
WE'RE GOING TO MAKE THIS SIMPLE. WHERE DID YOU UPLOAD THE FILES TO?
WHAT FILES?
I HAD A FEELING YOU WERE GOING TO SAY THAT.
SMAK
NOW, ONCE AGAIN... WHERE DID YOU UPLOAD THE FILES TO?
I HAVE NO IDEA WHAT YOU ARE TALKING ABOUT.
RIIII IIIIPP
I GUESS WE'RE GONNA HAVE TO GET CREATIVE...
HUH?
WHAT THE HELL IS THAT?

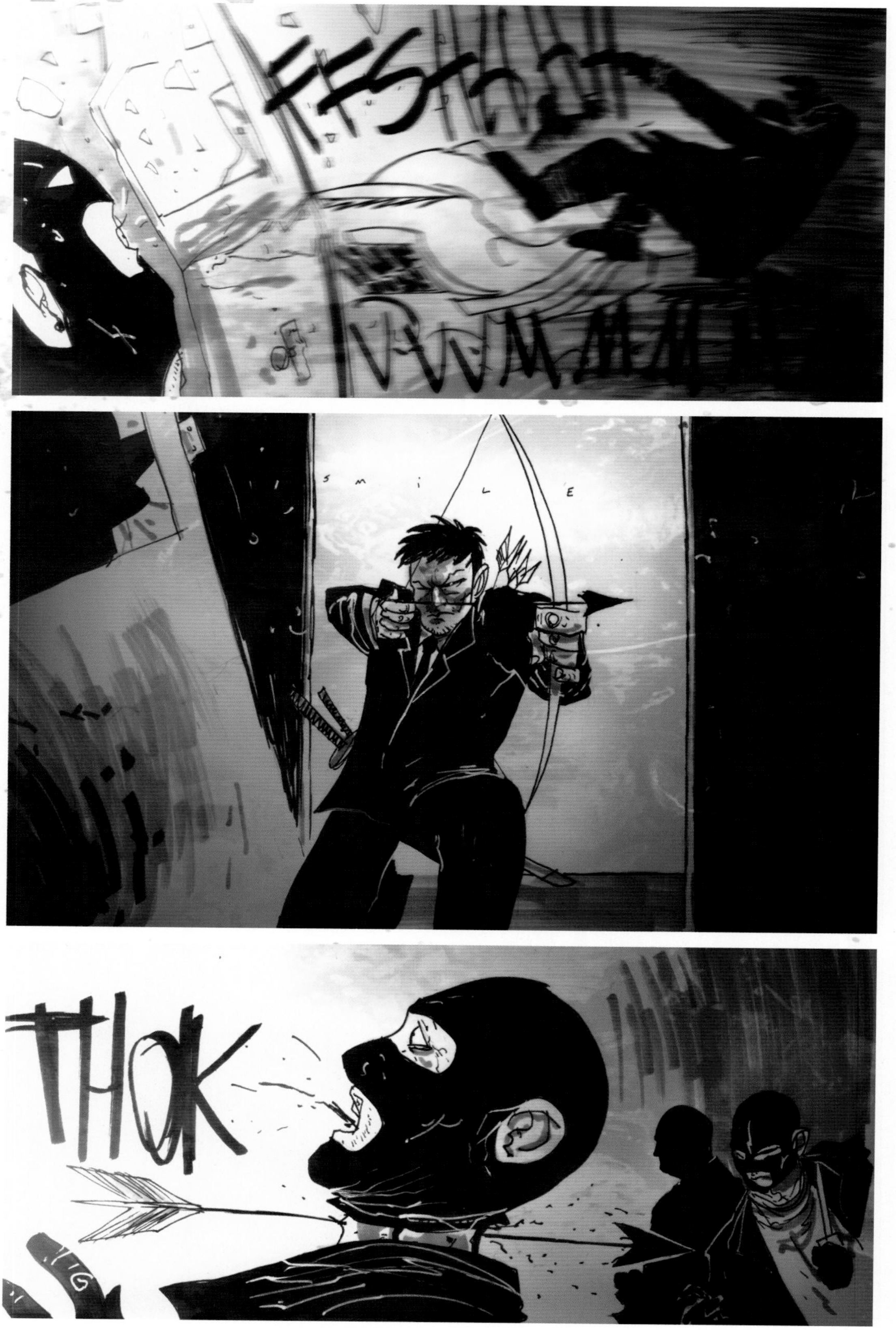
S M I L E
THOK

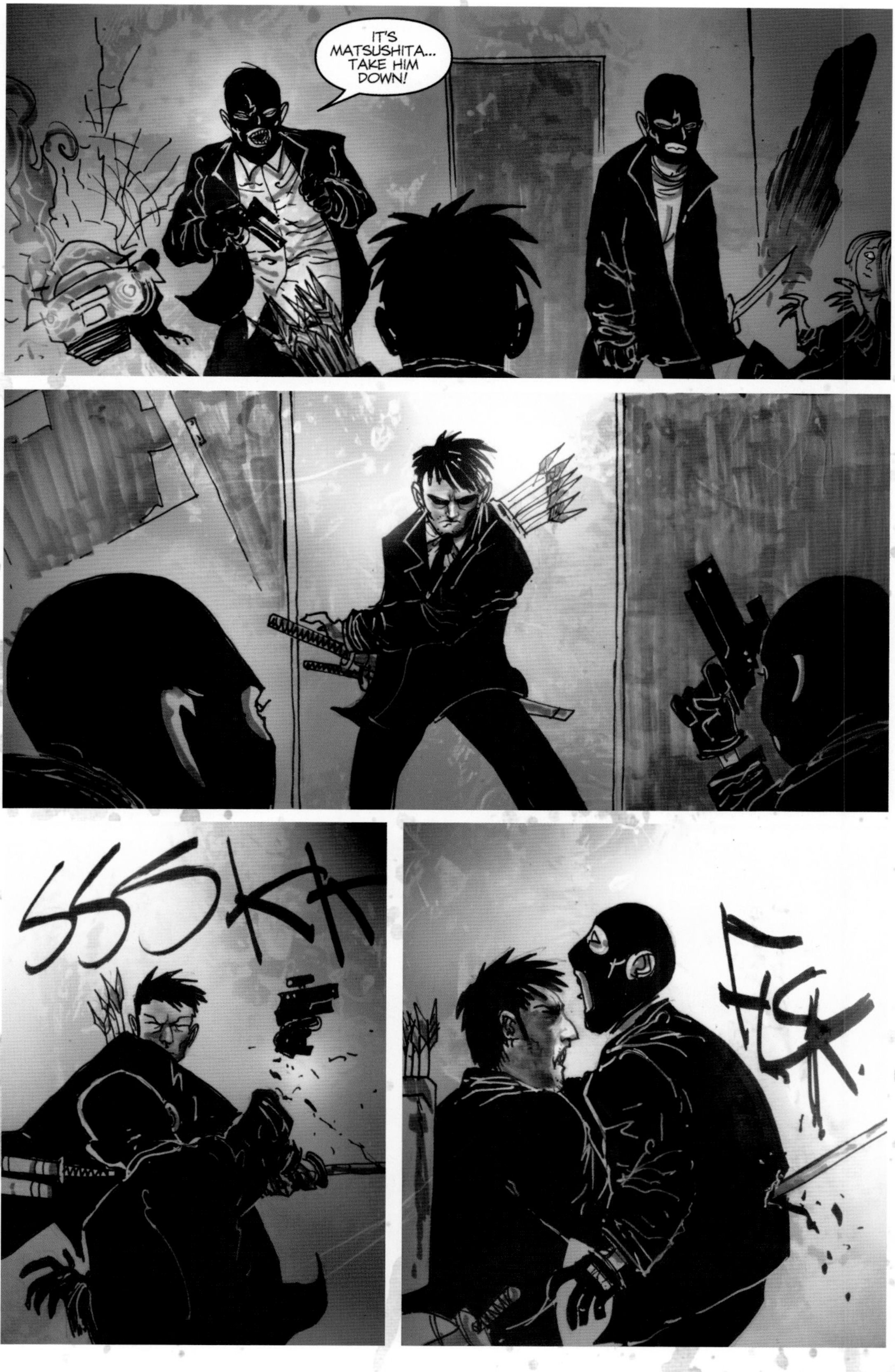
IT'S MATSUSHITA... TAKE HIM DOWN!

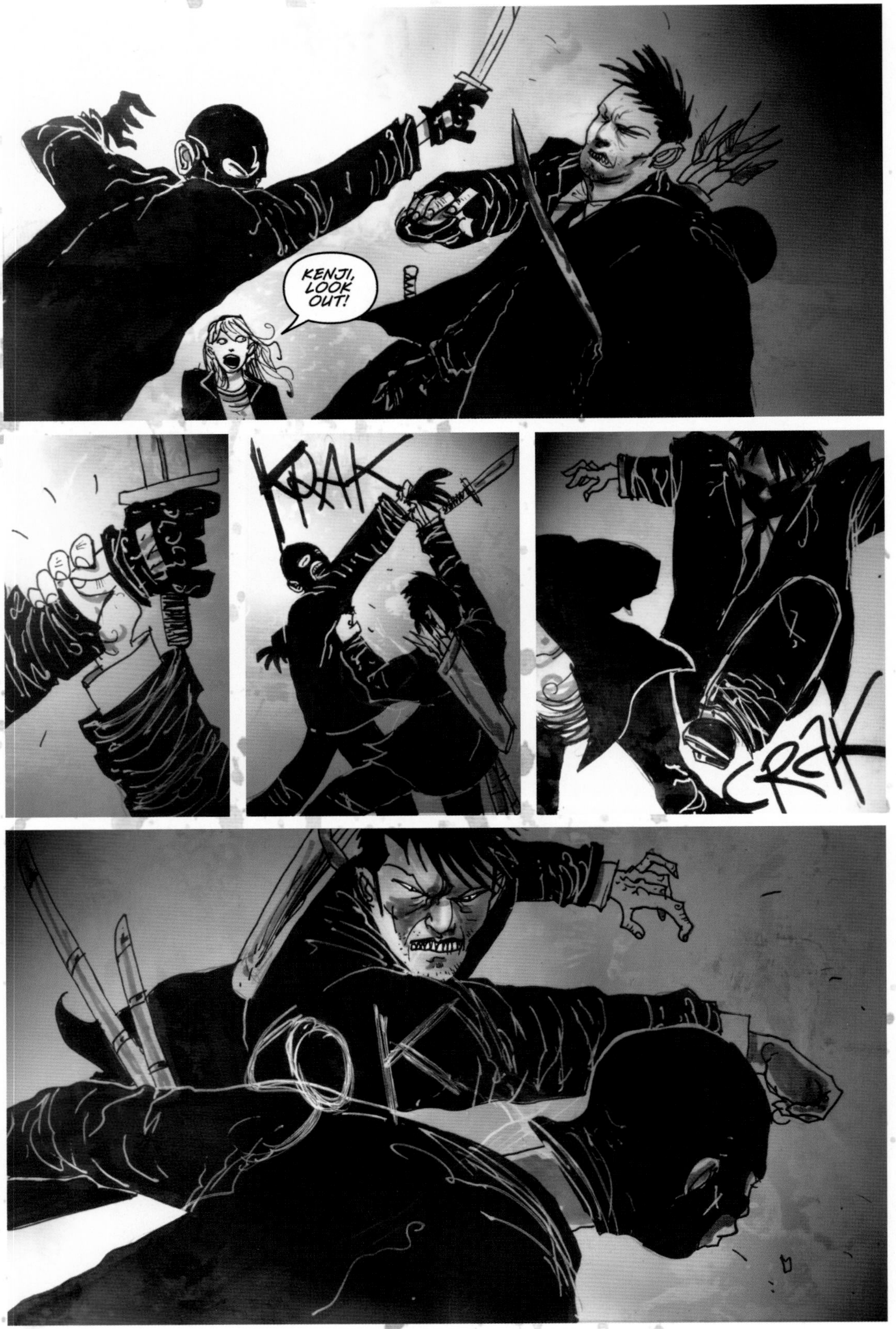
KENJI, LOOK OUT!
KRAK
CRACK

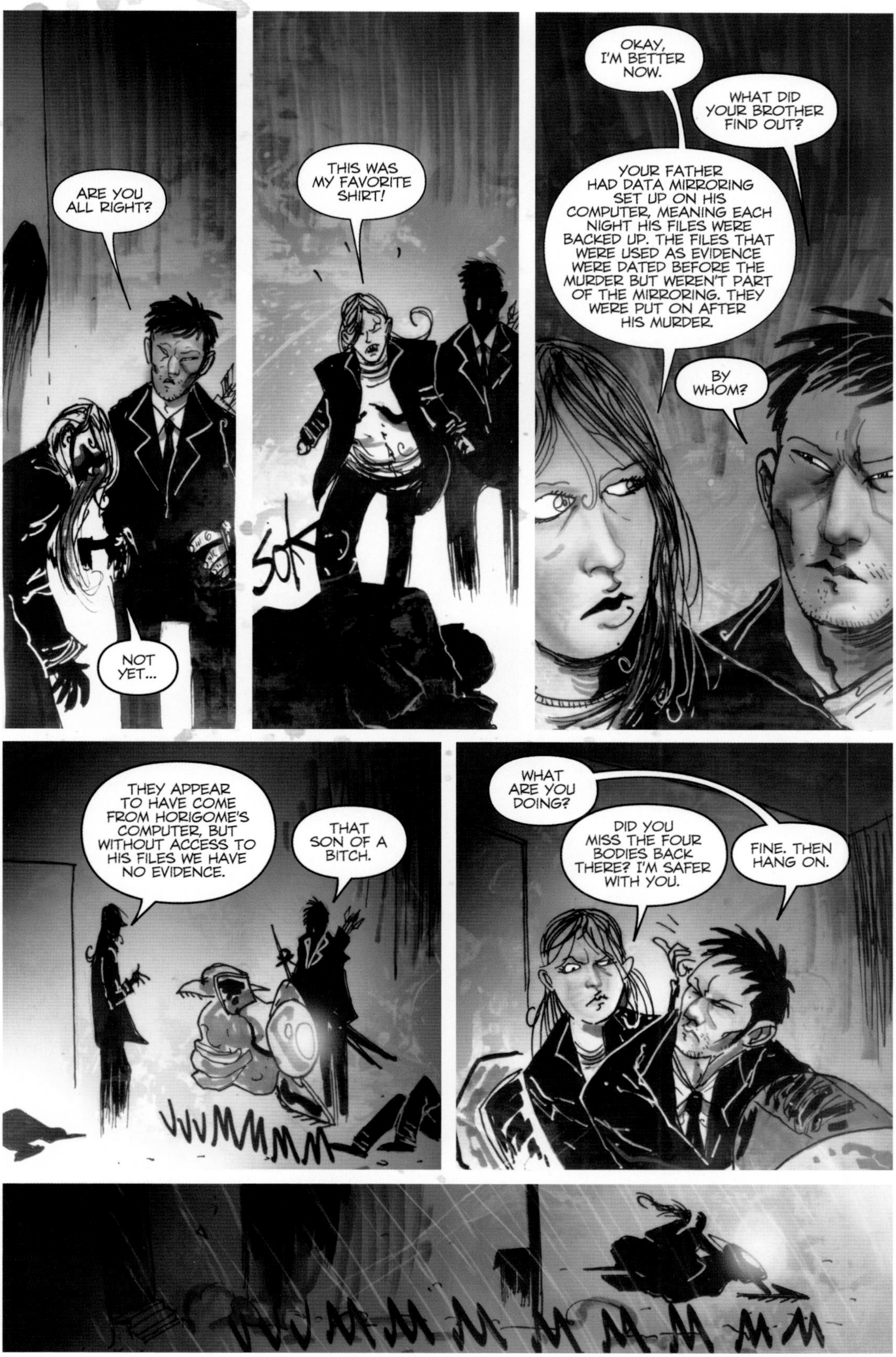
ARE YOU ALL RIGHT?
NOT YET...
THIS WAS MY FAVORITE SHIRT!
SOK
OKAY, I'M BETTER NOW.
WHAT DID YOUR BROTHER FIND OUT?
YOUR FATHER HAD DATA MIRRORING SET UP ON HIS COMPUTER, MEANING EACH NIGHT HIS FILES WERE BACKED UP. THE FILES THAT WERE USED AS EVIDENCE WERE DATED BEFORE THE MURDER BUT WEREN'T PART OF THE MIRRORING. THEY WERE PUT ON AFTER HIS MURDER.
BY WHOM?
THEY APPEAR TO HAVE COME FROM HORIGOME'S COMPUTER, BUT WITHOUT ACCESS TO HIS FILES WE HAVE NO EVIDENCE.
THAT SON OF A BITCH.
VVUMMMM
WHAT ARE YOU DOING?
DID YOU MISS THE FOUR BODIES BACK THERE? I'M SAFER WITH YOU.
FINE. THEN HANG ON.
VVUMMMMMMMMMMM

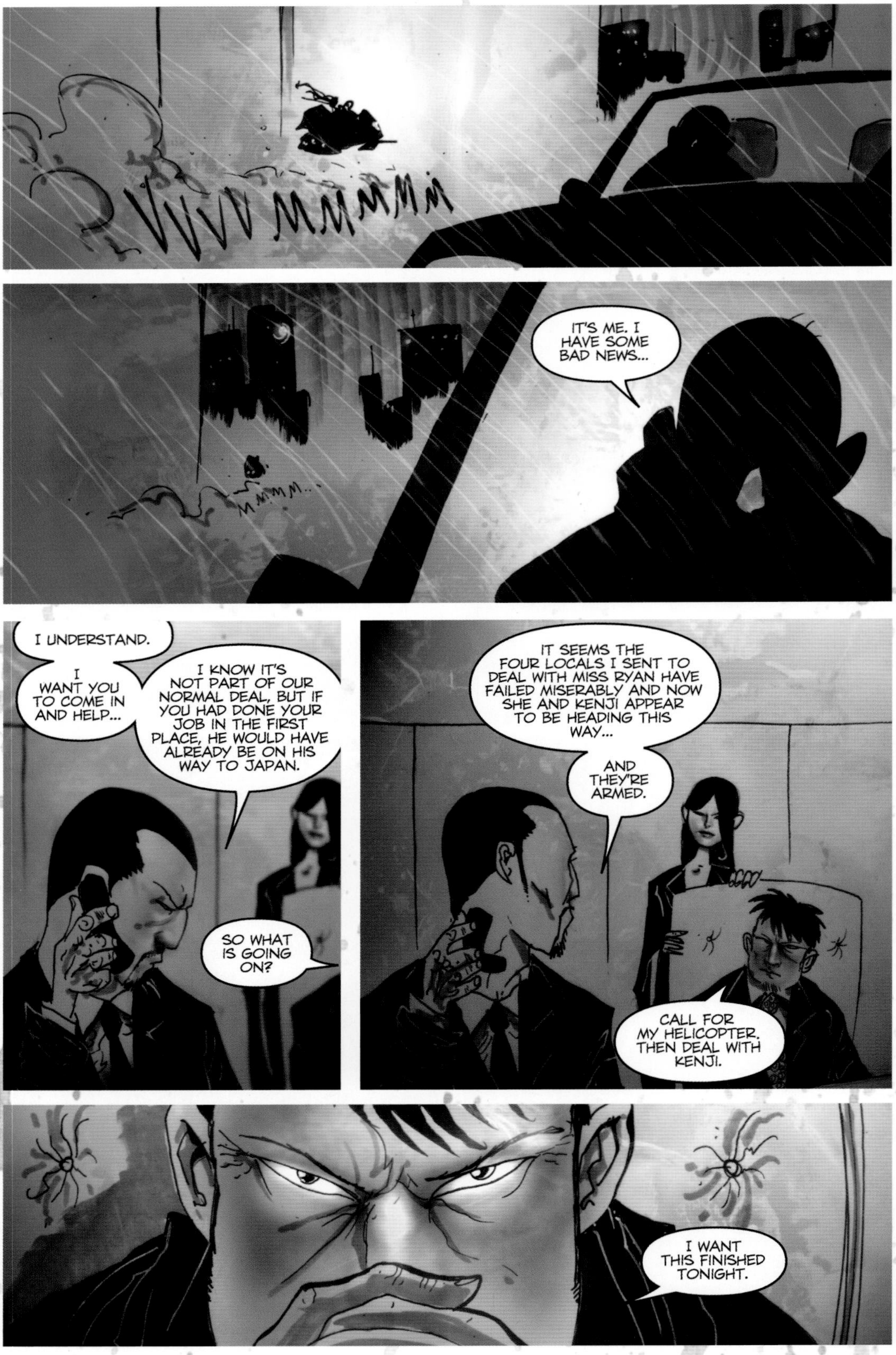

VVVVV MMMMM
IT'S ME. I HAVE SOME BAD NEWS...
MMMM...
I UNDERSTAND.
I WANT YOU TO COME IN AND HELP...
I KNOW IT'S NOT PART OF OUR NORMAL DEAL, BUT IF YOU HAD DONE YOUR JOB IN THE FIRST PLACE, HE WOULD HAVE ALREADY BE ON HIS WAY TO JAPAN.
SO WHAT IS GOING ON?
IT SEEMS THE FOUR LOCALS I SENT TO DEAL WITH MISS RYAN HAVE FAILED MISERABLY AND NOW SHE AND KENJI APPEAR TO BE HEADING THIS WAY...
AND THEY'RE ARMED.
CALL FOR MY HELICOPTER. THEN DEAL WITH KENJI.
I WANT THIS FINISHED TONIGHT.

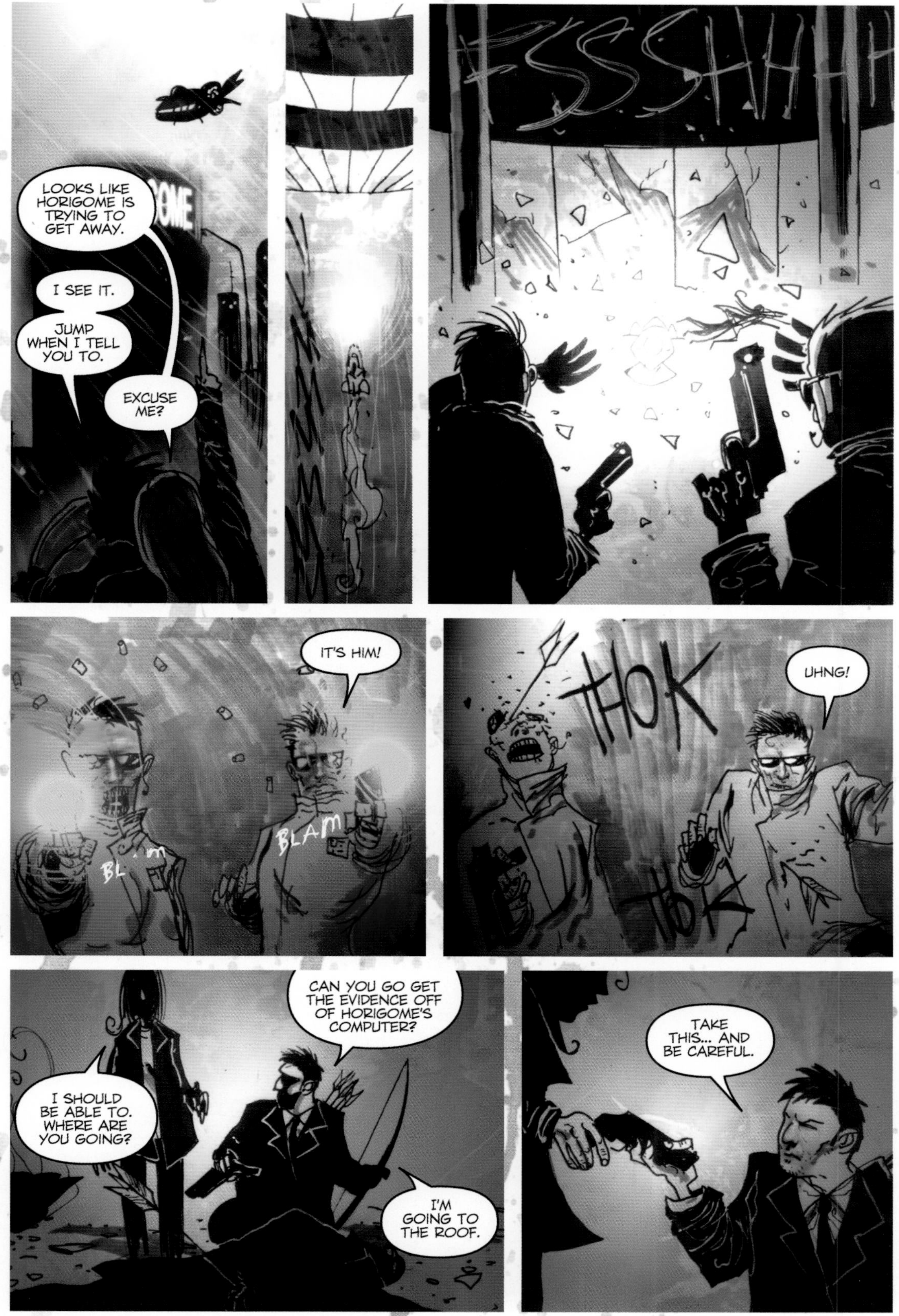
LOOKS LIKE HORIGOME IS TRYING TO GET AWAY.
I SEE IT.
JUMP WHEN I TELL YOU TO.
EXCUSE ME?
IT'S HIM!
BLAM
THOK
UHNG!
THOK
CAN YOU GO GET THE EVIDENCE OFF OF HORIGOME'S COMPUTER?
I SHOULD BE ABLE TO. WHERE ARE YOU GOING?
I'M GOING TO THE ROOF.
TAKE THIS... AND BE CAREFUL.

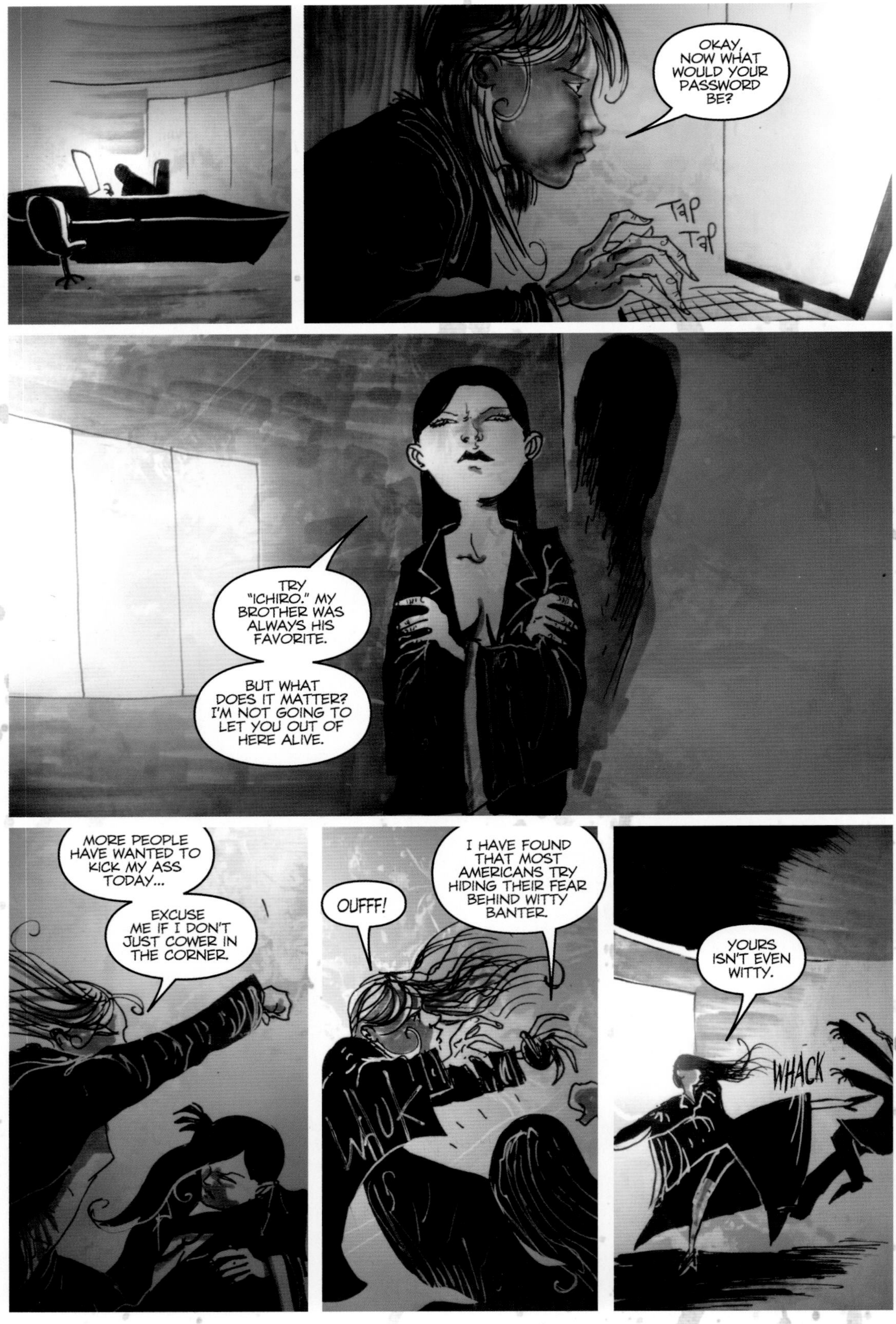
OKAY, NOW WHAT WOULD YOUR PASSWORD BE?
TAP TAP
TRY "ICHIRO." MY BROTHER WAS ALWAYS HIS FAVORITE.
BUT WHAT DOES IT MATTER? I'M NOT GOING TO LET YOU OUT OF HERE ALIVE.
MORE PEOPLE HAVE WANTED TO KICK MY ASS TODAY...
EXCUSE ME IF I DON'T JUST COWER IN THE CORNER.
OUFFF!
I HAVE FOUND THAT MOST AMERICANS TRY HIDING THEIR FEAR BEHIND WITTY BANTER.
WHUK
YOURS ISN'T EVEN WITTY.
WHACK

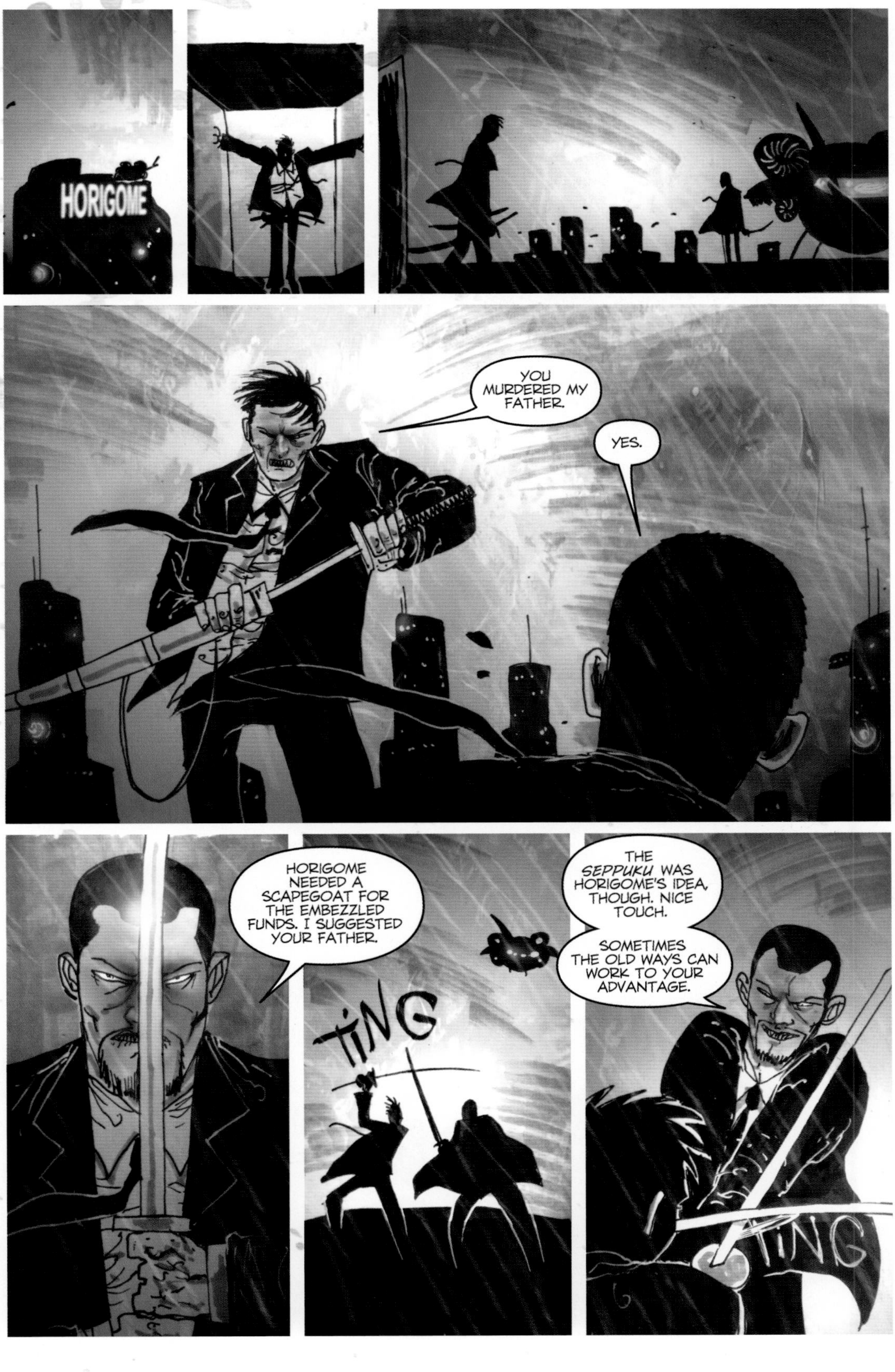
HORIGOME
YOU MURDERED MY FATHER.
YES.
HORIGOME NEEDED A SCAPEGOAT FOR THE EMBEZZLED FUNDS. I SUGGESTED YOUR FATHER.
TiNG
THE *SEPPUKU* WAS HORIGOME'S IDEA, THOUGH. NICE TOUCH.
SOMETIMES THE OLD WAYS CAN WORK TO YOUR ADVANTAGE.
TiNG

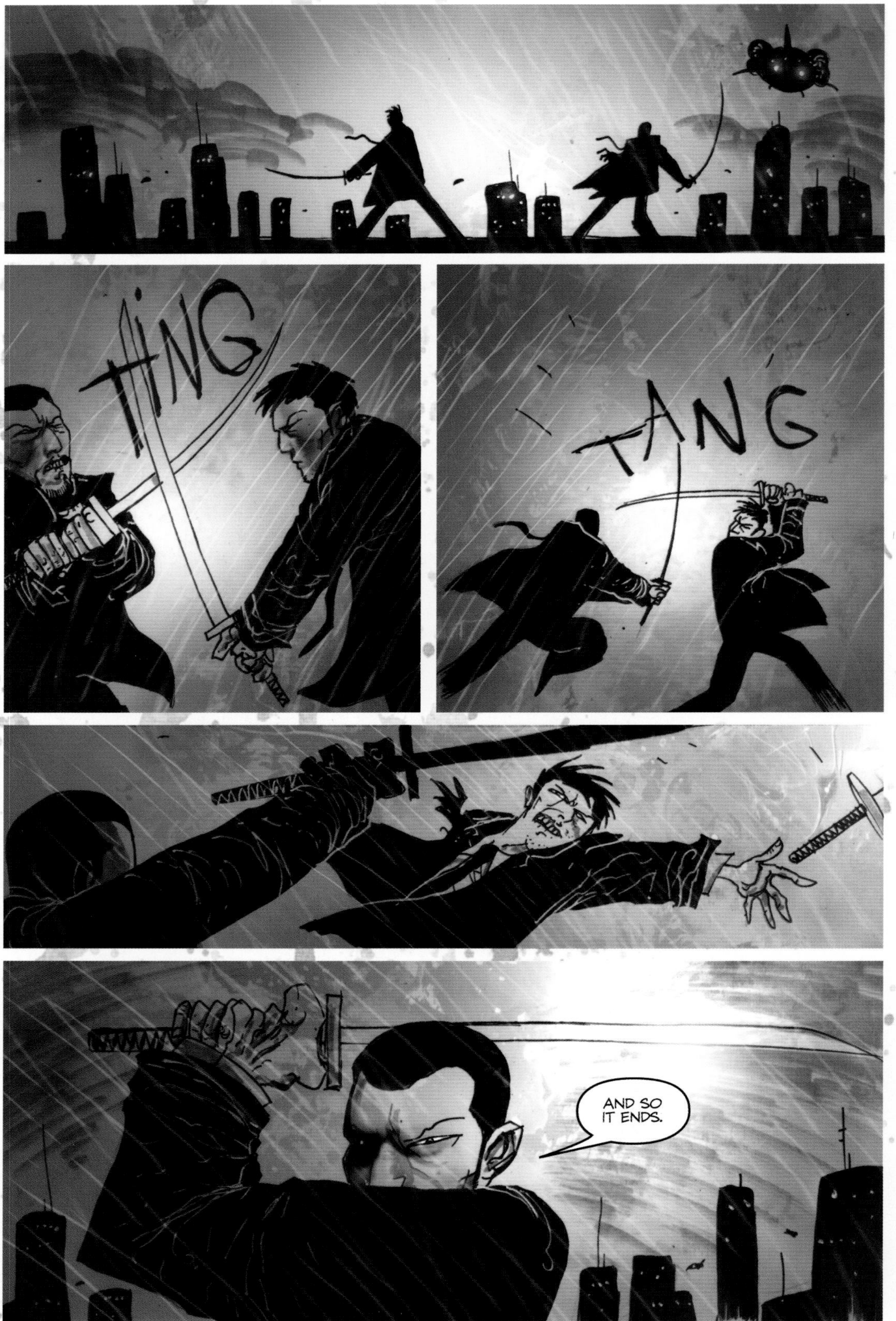
TING
TANG
AND SO IT ENDS.

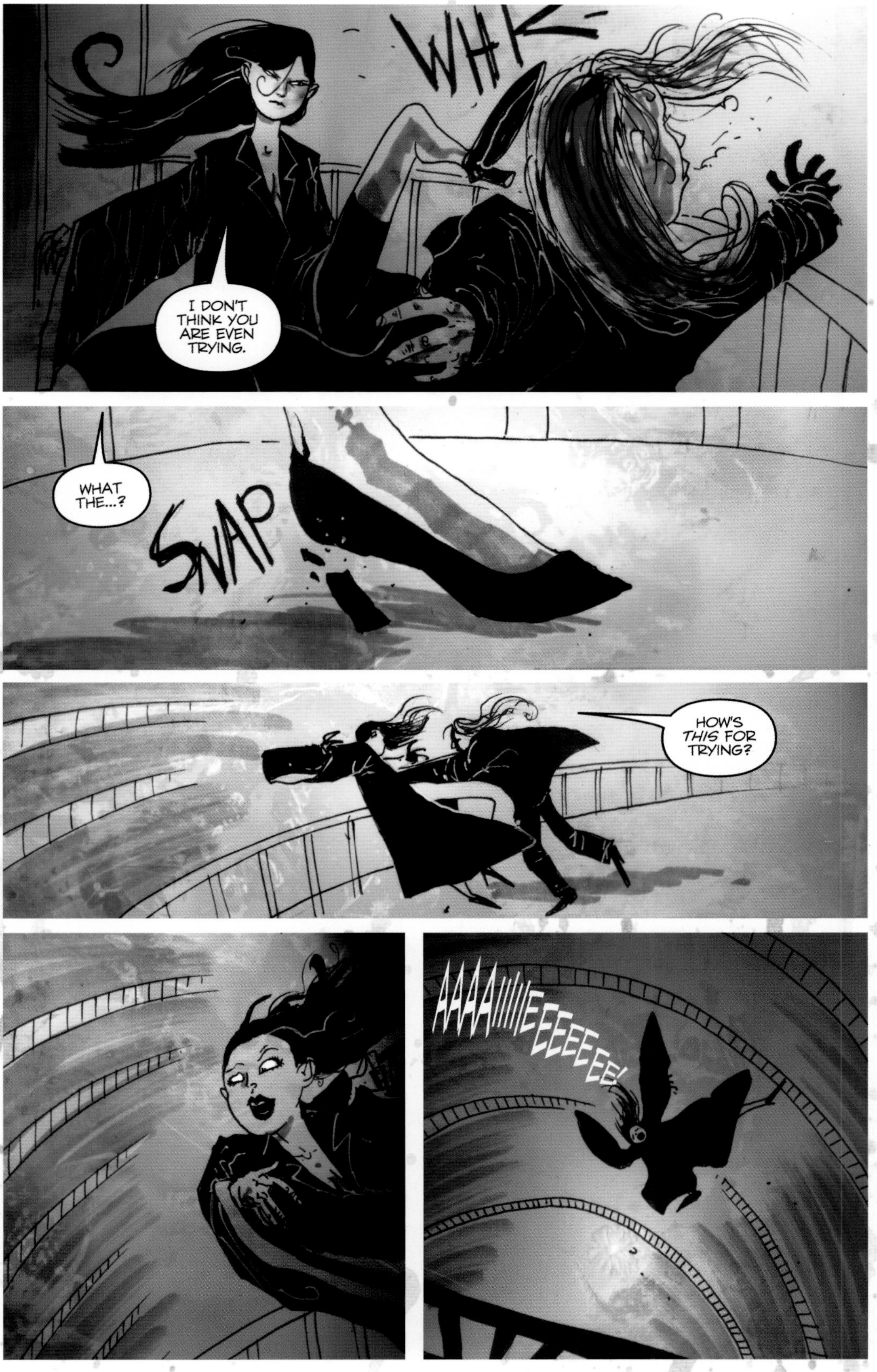
WHK-
I DON'T THINK YOU ARE EVEN TRYING.
WHAT THE...?
SNAP
HOW'S THIS FOR TRYING?
AAAAIIIIIEEEEEEE!

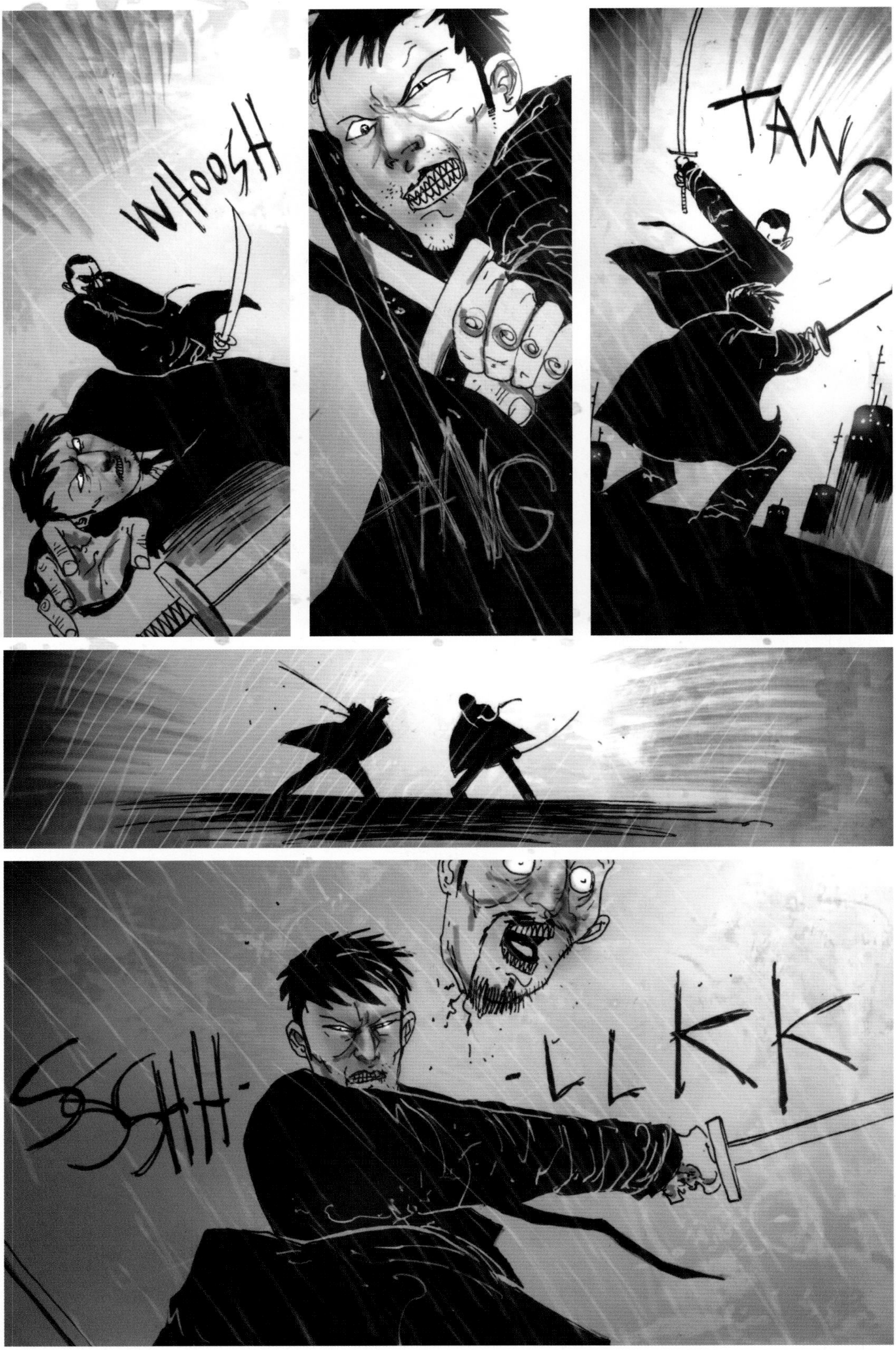

WHOOSH
TANG
TANG
SSCHH-
-LLKK

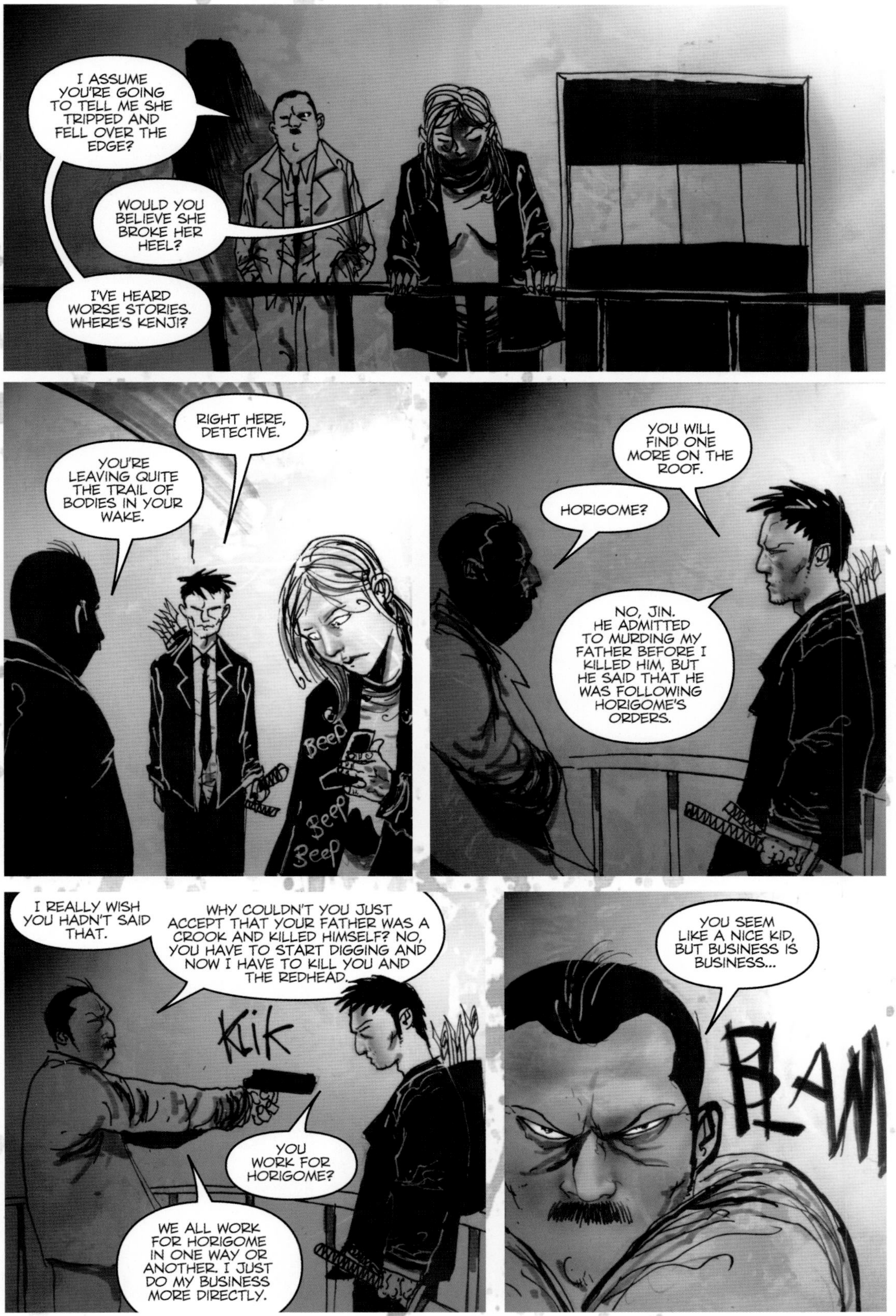

I ASSUME YOU'RE GOING TO TELL ME SHE TRIPPED AND FELL OVER THE EDGE?
WOULD YOU BELIEVE SHE BROKE HER HEEL?
I'VE HEARD WORSE STORIES. WHERE'S KENJI?
YOU'RE LEAVING QUITE THE TRAIL OF BODIES IN YOUR WAKE.
RIGHT HERE, DETECTIVE.
Beep
Beep
Beep
HORIGOME?
YOU WILL FIND ONE MORE ON THE ROOF.
NO, JIN. HE ADMITTED TO MURDING MY FATHER BEFORE I KILLED HIM, BUT HE SAID THAT HE WAS FOLLOWING HORIGOME'S ORDERS.
I REALLY WISH YOU HADN'T SAID THAT.
WHY COULDN'T YOU JUST ACCEPT THAT YOUR FATHER WAS A CROOK AND KILLED HIMSELF? NO, YOU HAVE TO START DIGGING AND NOW I HAVE TO KILL YOU AND THE REDHEAD.
KLIK
YOU WORK FOR HORIGOME?
WE ALL WORK FOR HORIGOME IN ONE WAY OR ANOTHER. I JUST DO MY BUSINESS MORE DIRECTLY.
YOU SEEM LIKE A NICE KID, BUT BUSINESS IS BUSINESS...
BLAM

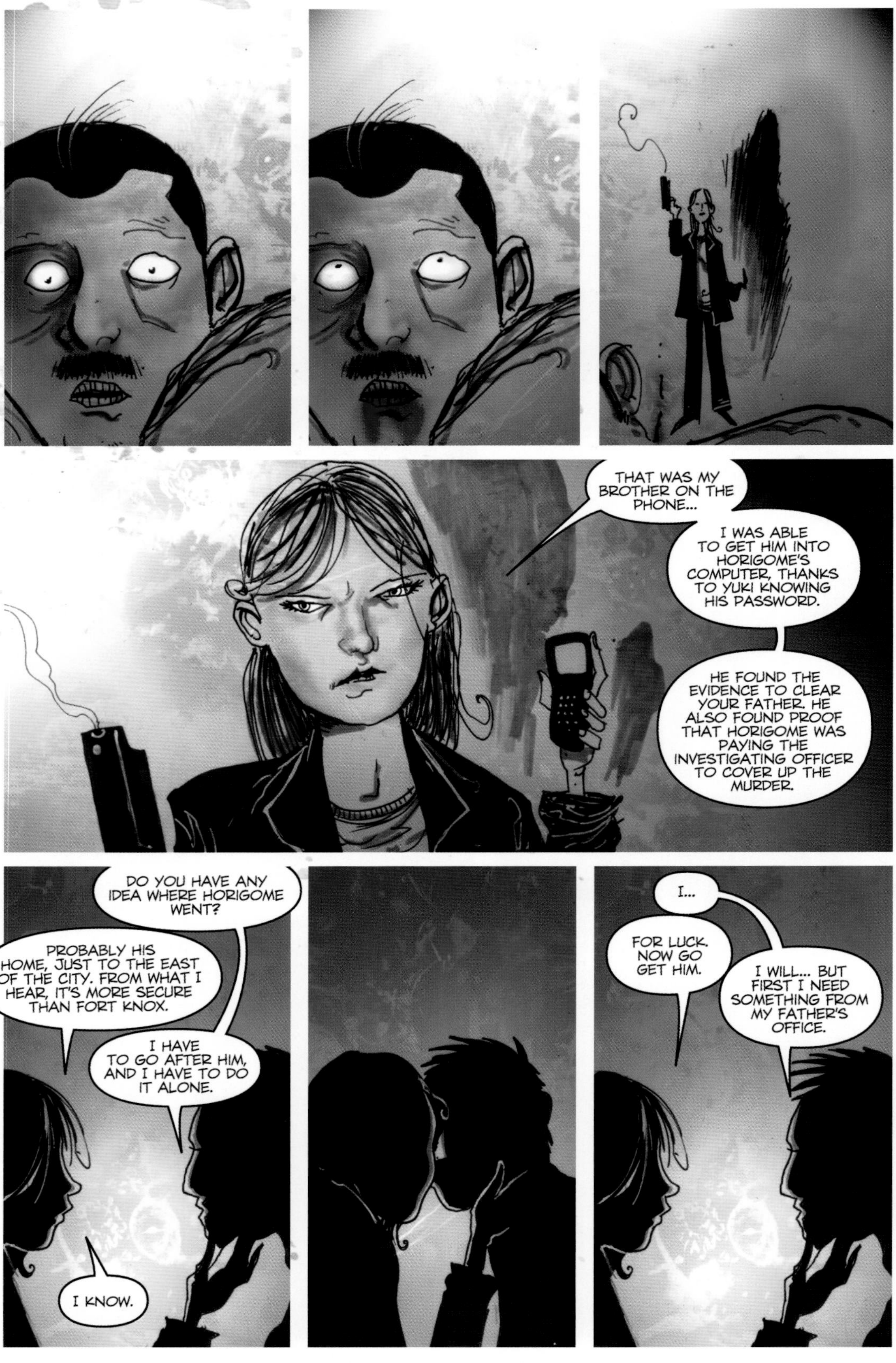
THAT WAS MY BROTHER ON THE PHONE...
I WAS ABLE TO GET HIM INTO HORIGOME'S COMPUTER, THANKS TO YUKI KNOWING HIS PASSWORD.
HE FOUND THE EVIDENCE TO CLEAR YOUR FATHER. HE ALSO FOUND PROOF THAT HORIGOME WAS PAYING THE INVESTIGATING OFFICER TO COVER UP THE MURDER.
DO YOU HAVE ANY IDEA WHERE HORIGOME WENT?
PROBABLY HIS HOME, JUST TO THE EAST OF THE CITY. FROM WHAT I HEAR, IT'S MORE SECURE THAN FORT KNOX.
I HAVE TO GO AFTER HIM, AND I HAVE TO DO IT ALONE.
I KNOW.
I...
FOR LUCK. NOW GO GET HIM.
I WILL... BUT FIRST I NEED SOMETHING FROM MY FATHER'S OFFICE.

CLK
TKK

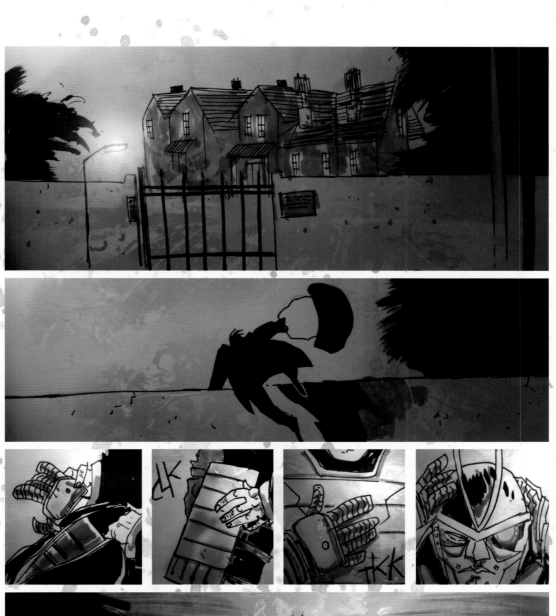

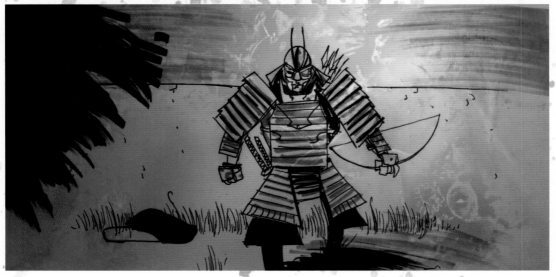

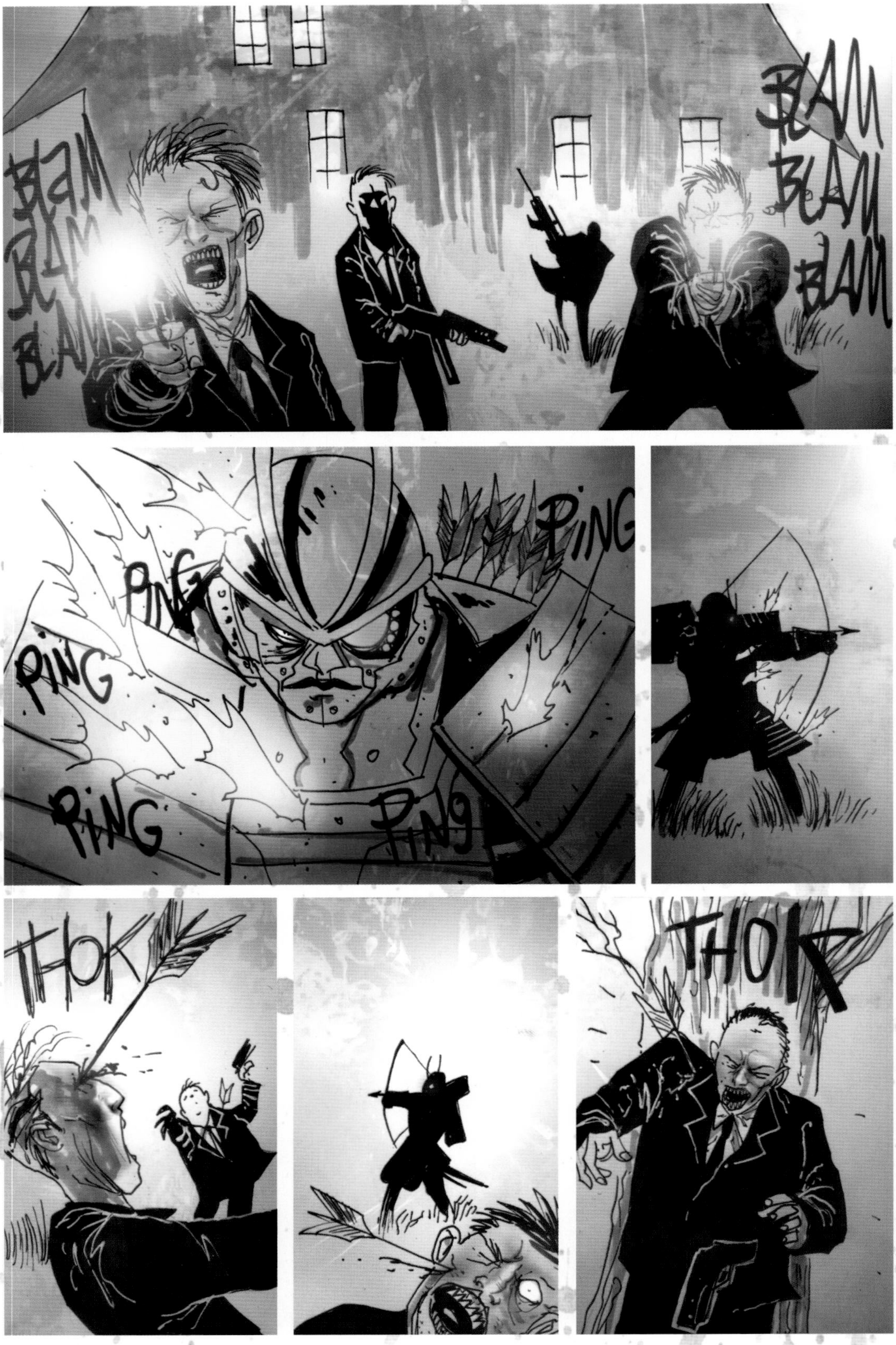
BLAM BLAM BLAM BLAM
BLAM BLAM BLAM
PING
PING
PING
PING
PING
THOK
THOK

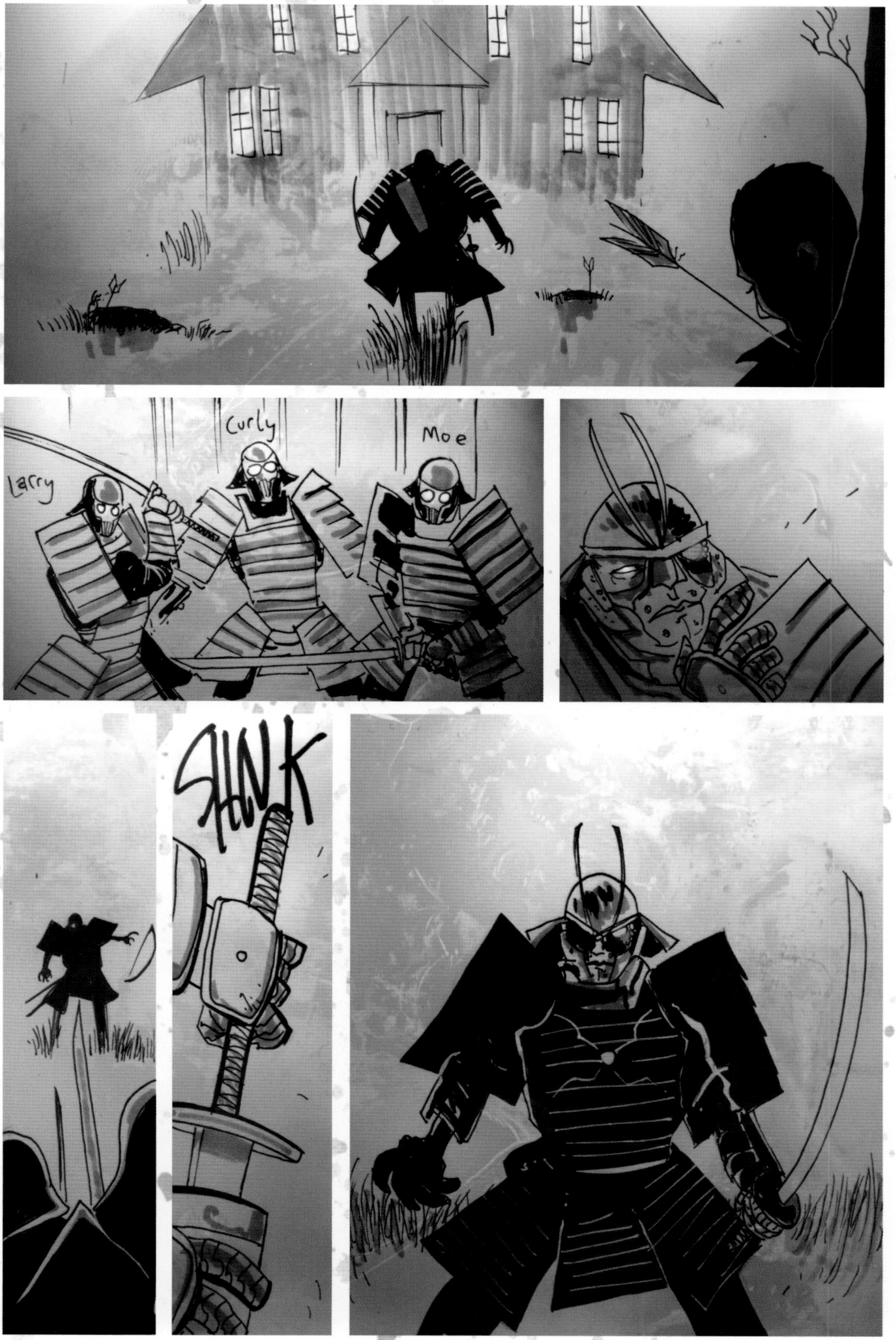
Larry
Curly
Moe
SHUNK

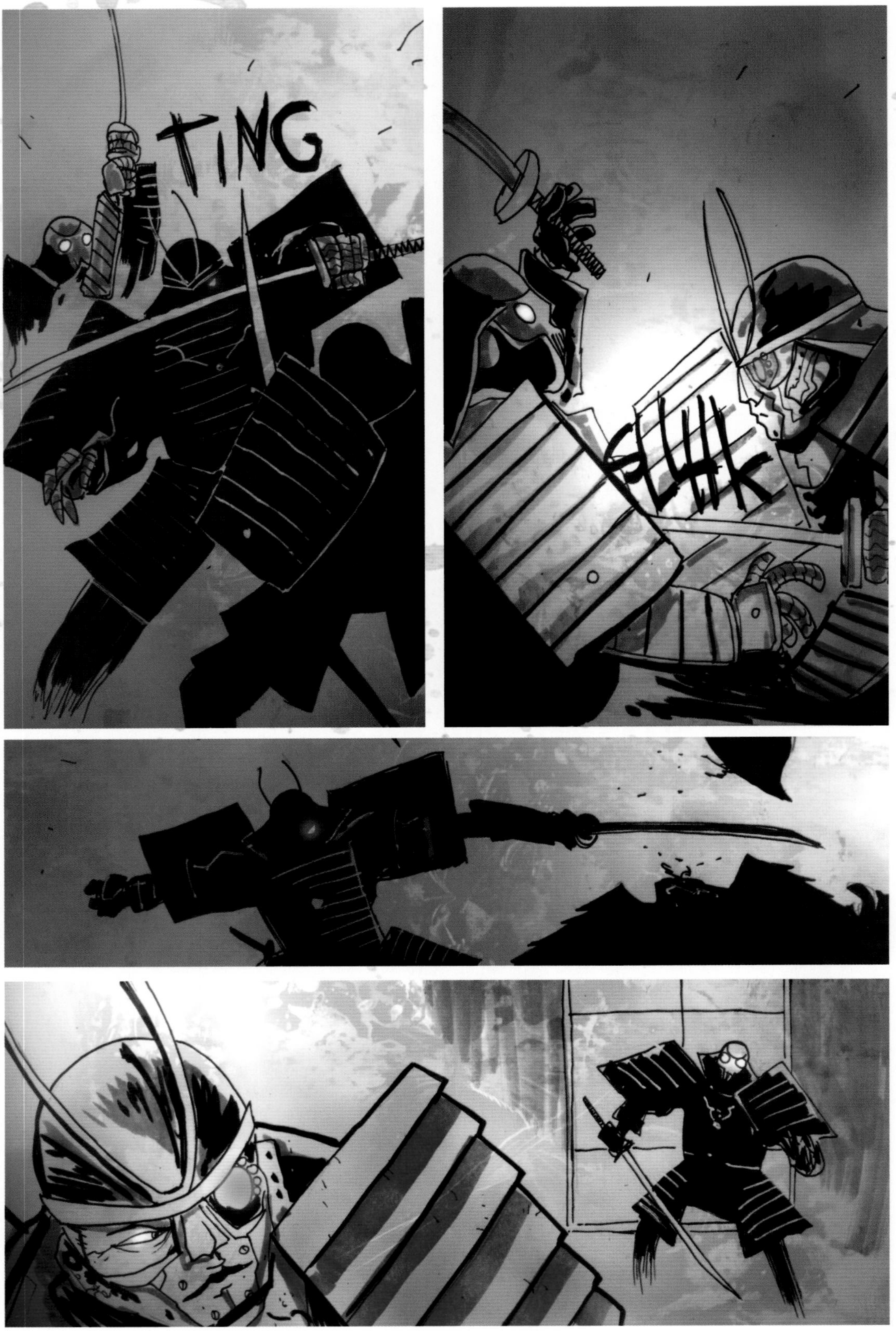
TING
SLUHK

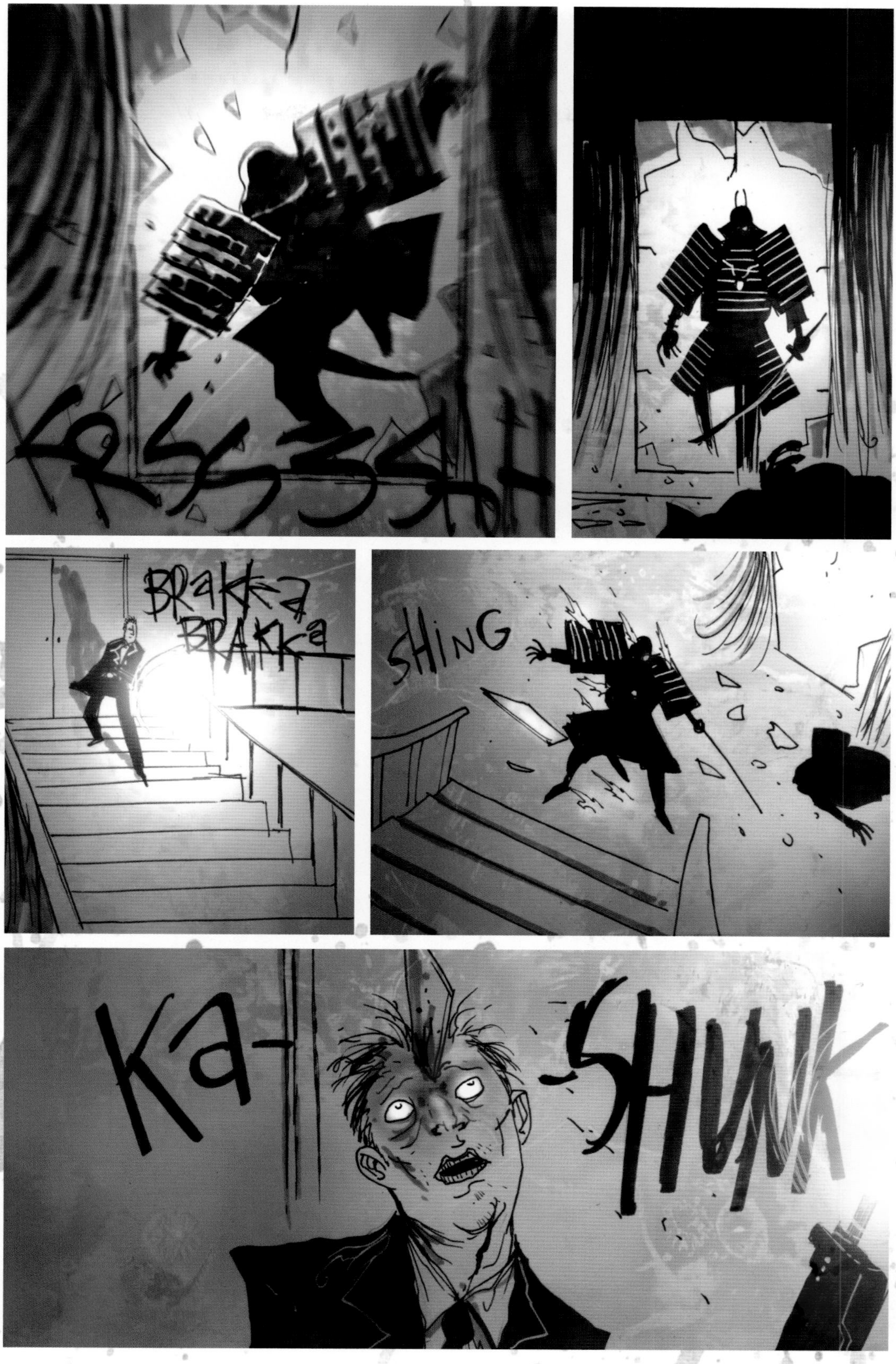
KRSSSSHH
BRAKKA
BRAKKA
SHING
KA-
SHUNK

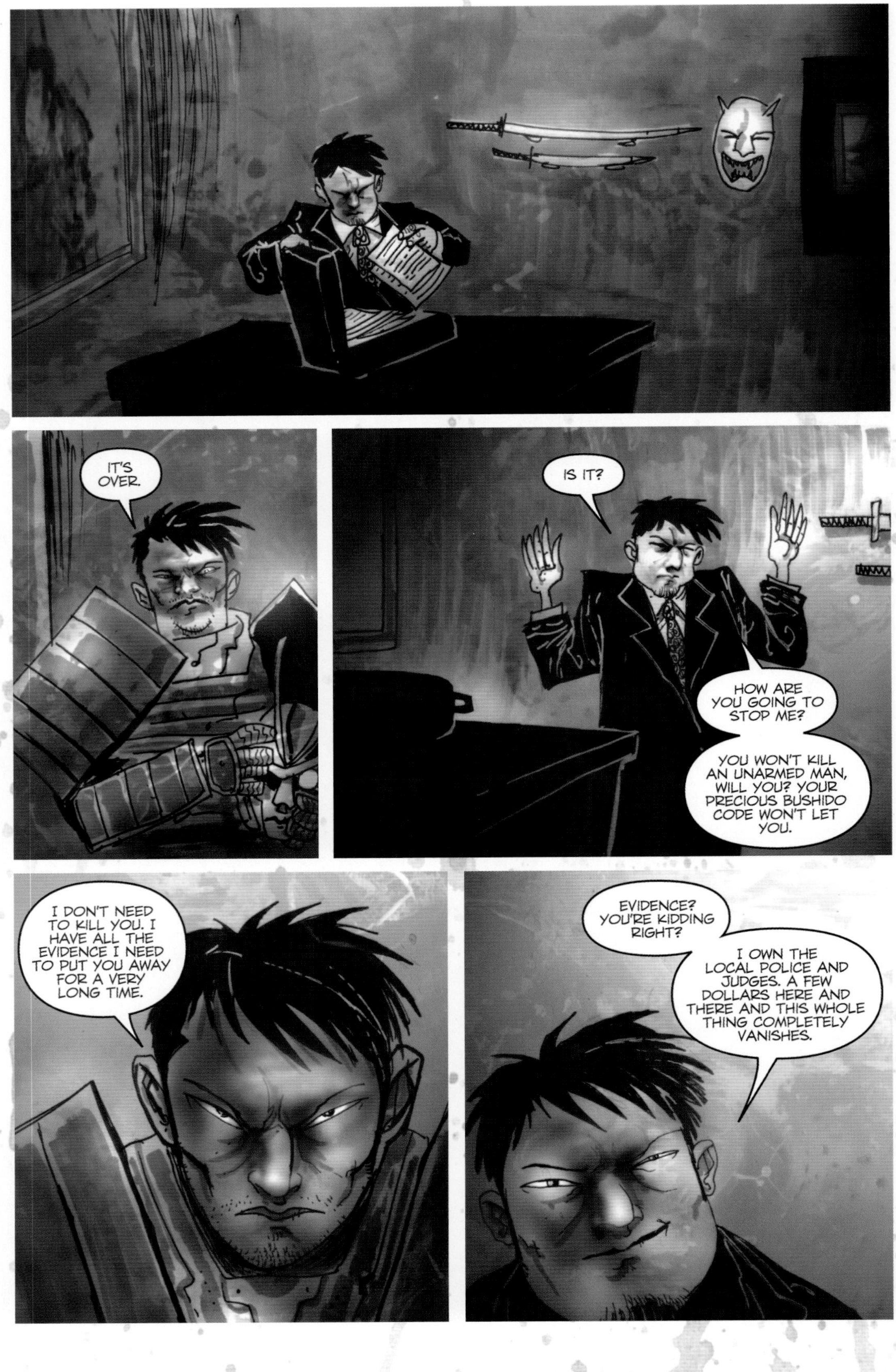
IT'S OVER.
IS IT?
HOW ARE YOU GOING TO STOP ME?
YOU WON'T KILL AN UNARMED MAN, WILL YOU? YOUR PRECIOUS BUSHIDO CODE WON'T LET YOU.
I DON'T NEED TO KILL YOU. I HAVE ALL THE EVIDENCE I NEED TO PUT YOU AWAY FOR A VERY LONG TIME.
EVIDENCE? YOU'RE KIDDING RIGHT?
I OWN THE LOCAL POLICE AND JUDGES. A FEW DOLLARS HERE AND THERE AND THIS WHOLE THING COMPLETELY VANISHES.

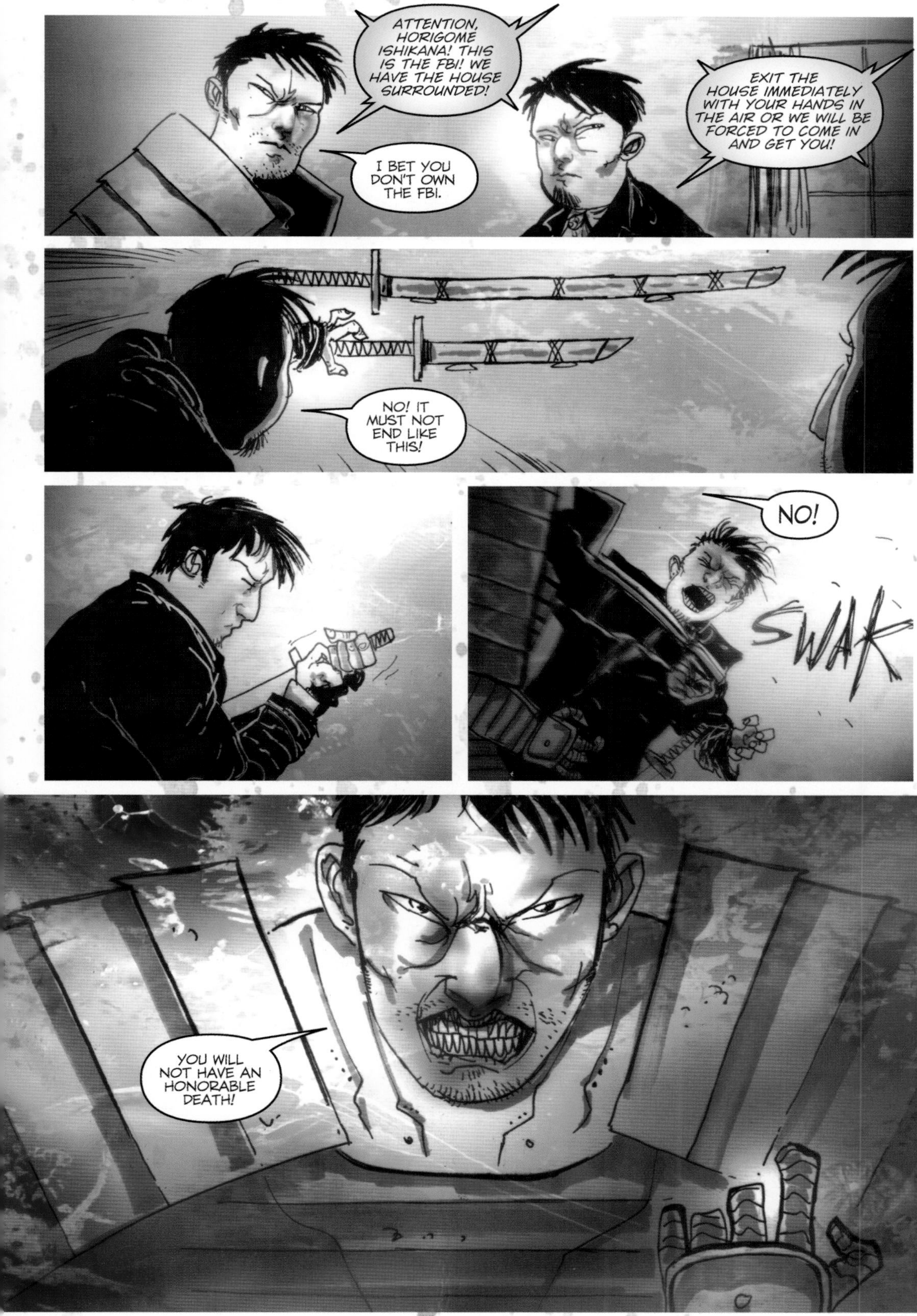
ATTENTION, HORIGOME ISHIKANA! THIS IS THE FBI! WE HAVE THE HOUSE SURROUNDED!
I BET YOU DON'T OWN THE FBI.
EXIT THE HOUSE IMMEDIATELY WITH YOUR HANDS IN THE AIR OR WE WILL BE FORCED TO COME IN AND GET YOU!
NO! IT MUST NOT END LIKE THIS!
NO!
SWAK
YOU WILL NOT HAVE AN HONORABLE DEATH!

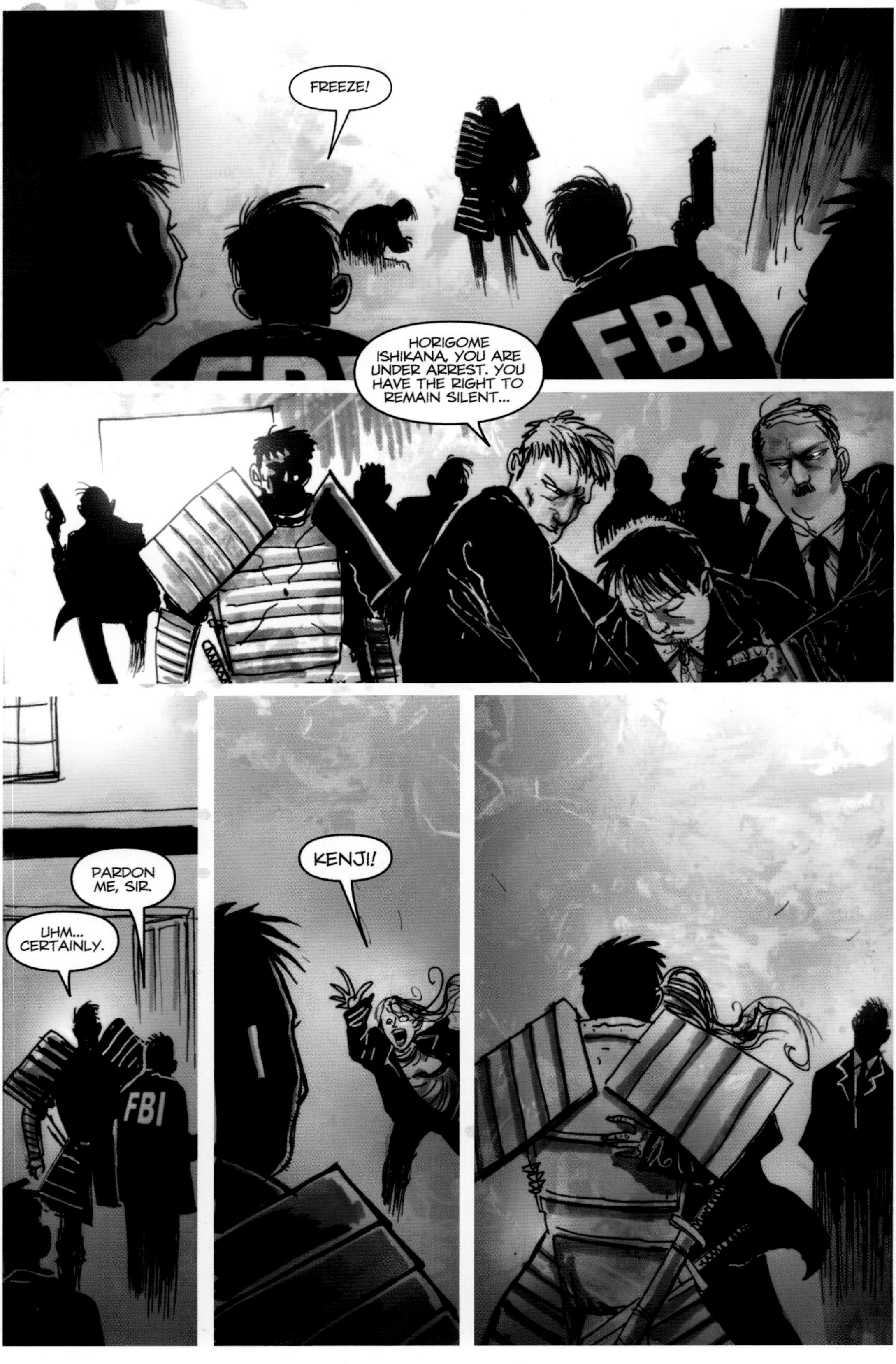
FREEZE!
FBI
FBI
HORIGOME ISHIKANA, YOU ARE UNDER ARREST. YOU HAVE THE RIGHT TO REMAIN SILENT...
PARDON ME, SIR.
UHM... CERTAINLY.
FBI
KENJI!

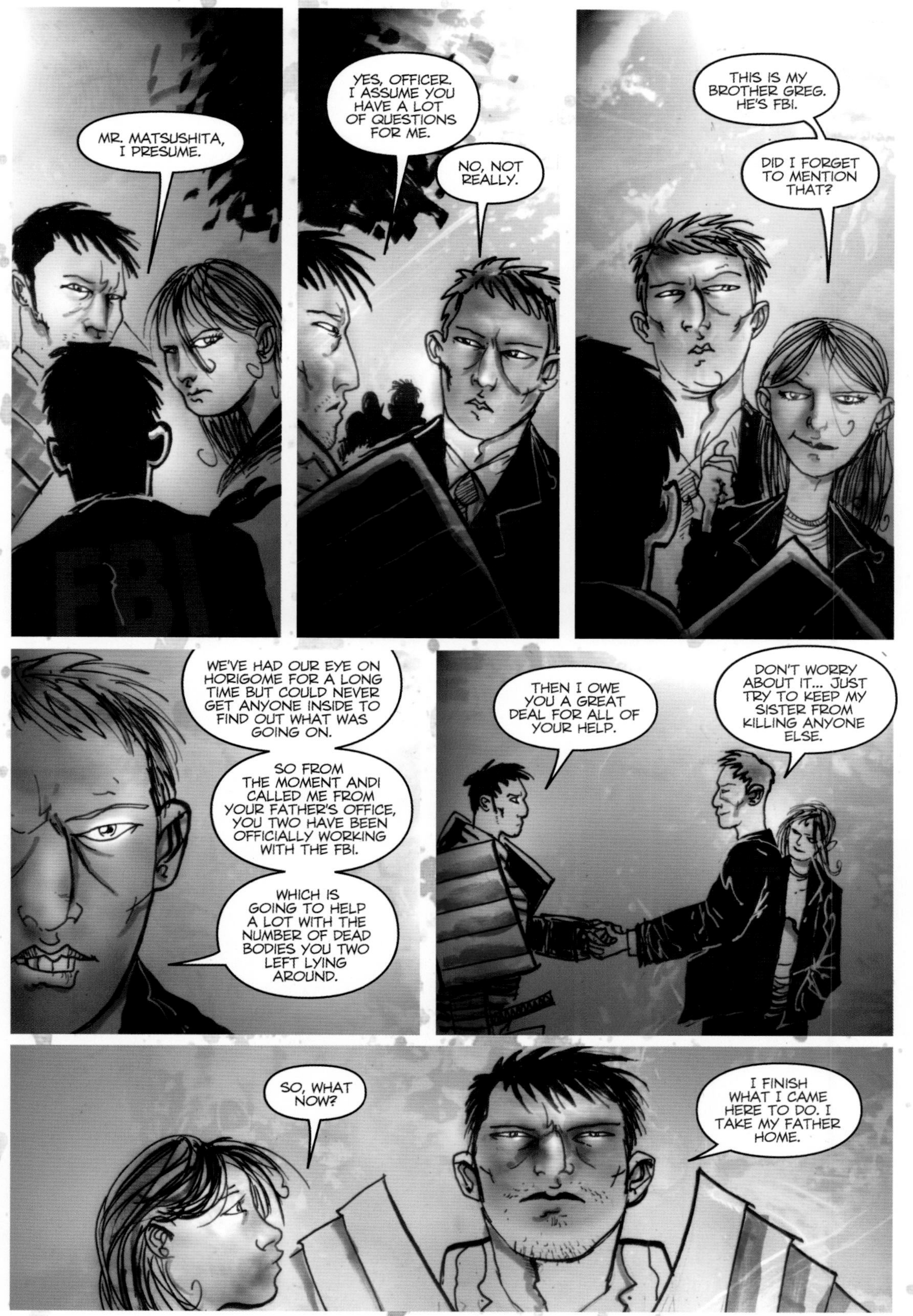
MR. MATSUSHITA, I PRESUME.
YES, OFFICER. I ASSUME YOU HAVE A LOT OF QUESTIONS FOR ME.
NO, NOT REALLY.
THIS IS MY BROTHER GREG. HE'S FBI.
DID I FORGET TO MENTION THAT?
FBI
WE'VE HAD OUR EYE ON HORIGOME FOR A LONG TIME BUT COULD NEVER GET ANYONE INSIDE TO FIND OUT WHAT WAS GOING ON.
SO FROM THE MOMENT ANDI CALLED ME FROM YOUR FATHER'S OFFICE, YOU TWO HAVE BEEN OFFICIALLY WORKING WITH THE FBI.
WHICH IS GOING TO HELP A LOT WITH THE NUMBER OF DEAD BODIES YOU TWO LEFT LYING AROUND.
THEN I OWE YOU A GREAT DEAL FOR ALL OF YOUR HELP.
DON'T WORRY ABOUT IT... JUST TRY TO KEEP MY SISTER FROM KILLING ANYONE ELSE.
SO, WHAT NOW?
I FINISH WHAT I CAME HERE TO DO. I TAKE MY FATHER HOME.

VERY FEW BELIEVE IN THE WAYS OF THE PAST OR FOLLOW THE CODE. BUT YOU EMBRACED IT AND MADE IT YOUR WAY OF LIFE.

HONOR ABOVE ALL ELSE.

YOU LEARNED THAT FROM YOUR FATHER AND PASSED IT ON TO ME.

"YOU LIVED YOUR LIFE WITH HONOR.

"YOU HAVE DIED WITH HONOR."

AND YOU SHALL BE LAID TO REST WITH YOUR SWORD...

...STAINED WITH THE BLOOD OF YOUR KILLER

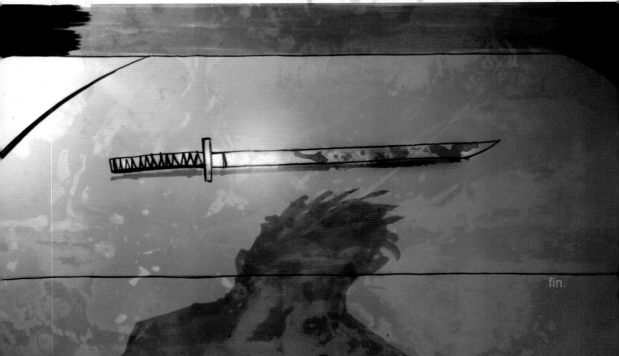

fin.